Flux Designer Toys

Designed and edited by Shawn Wright
Associate Editor Brigida Neves

Gingko press

Introduction

Ever changing, challenging and re-Inventing; designer toys are in a never-ending state of flux. Old becomes new and new can become pioneering.

From trailblazers broadening the scope of character based designer toys to the latest new talents making their name in the industry, this book will introduce you to some of the most skilled artists of their genre.

Take an intimate and exciting journey through the idiosyncrasies of designer playthings. Every artist featured offers you the chance to meet the quirky characters of their imagination, and see the world through their eyes and by their words.

And it's not just toys. This book is bursting at the seams with inspiration. The supporting artwork of the designers tells the story of the characters' development. You're shown how the paper sketch of a good character can make it cross media through vinyl, advertising, animation, illustration, cloth design, and much more.
This title also presents exclusive new works and tip offs on what to look out for in the future.
"Flux Designer Toys" doesn't just show you the characters and art work from designers worldwide. It gives the reader a glimpse of the thoughts and aims of the person behind the art.

Designed by : Shawn Wright
Edited by : Shawn Wright and Brigida Neves
Special thanks to Georja Calvi Smith a.k.a big Georja

Contents

Jon Burgerman

From the UK, Jon Burgerman has been working in the arts for 8 years. Although he enjoys experimenting, his preferred media is black pen on white paper: "Simple, quick and satisfying".

Most of all he aims "to encourage play and the exploration of narrative by the user." when he creates.

Burgerman prefers to use the simplest and easiest route to realize his works. As he puts it, "It's not the method that will determine how special the end result will be, only the finished work."

Ideas and concepts are generated through what he reads, thinks and observes; which then filter into his brain and eventually help generate ideas.

"If my work is successful on any level it will register an emotive response from the viewer."

Photographs by: Nathan Beddows

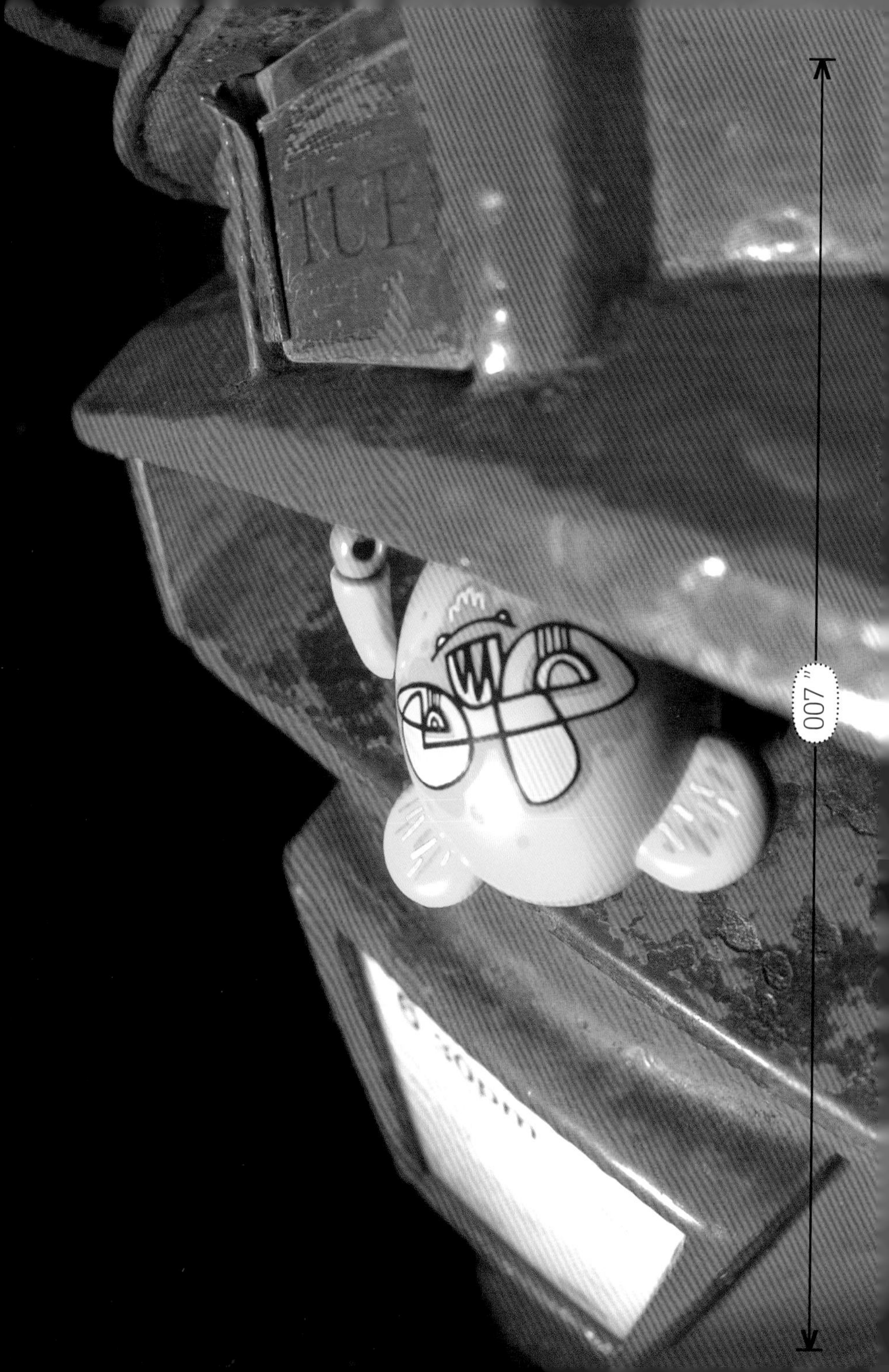

What's The Skinny

Clients and projects you last worked on?

I've produced clothing lines for Size and RipCurl, a book for ROJO and I am working on another one for IdN. I've designed a can for Pepsi. Recently I worked on lots of other cool projects too, but I can't remember them all right now!

Is there a message in your work or an issue that you want or try to address?

Messages can change from project to project. Overall I like to explore notions of confusion, worship, consumption and expectations.
These are things I think about a lot and am trying to work out for myself, so they come through in my work.

What do you enjoy about your work?

I enjoy being able to explore ideas, thoughts and idle musings through drawing, color and shapes.
Making the work can often be the most exciting part of the process. I like it when people say they enjoy the work, of course, but I never really know how to react to it-it feels a little embarrassing sometimes.

Where do you find your inspiration?

Everywhere!

Spicy Brown

Based in Los Angeles, California, Spicy Brown started "cookin" in 2003. It started from scratch with talented designers, artists, friends and family.

Contributing members come from leading fashion, toy, and design companies, whilst Spicy Brown's company policy assures that every artist retains full control and ownership of the artwork they create specifically for them.

Working mostly with T-shirts and designer toys, Spicy Brown tells us that the main aim of their products is "to make you hungry and smile!"

"The art should be the voice and message.
Each viewer will get their own meaning from it. Just enjoy it."

Photos by Junko Natsumi

Designed by Sachiho Hino and Kazuko Shinoka

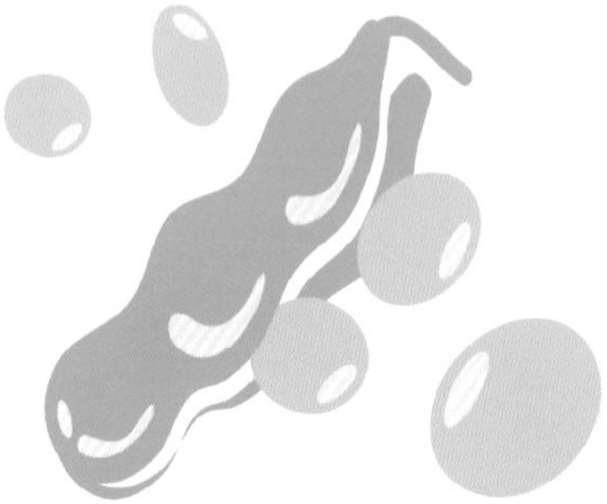

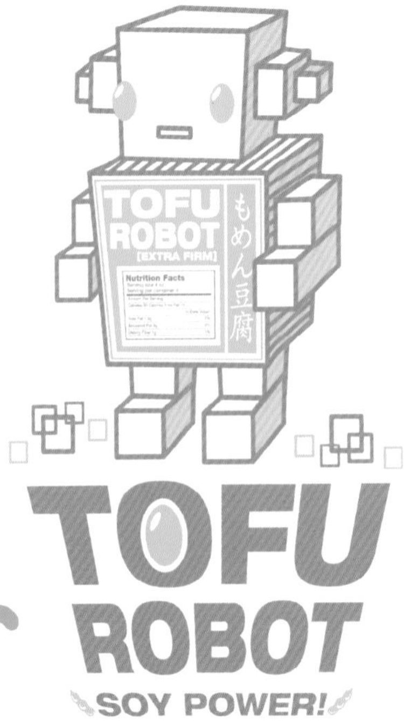

TOFU
ROBOT
もめん豆腐

TOFU
ROBOT
[EXTRA FIRM]
Nutrition Facts

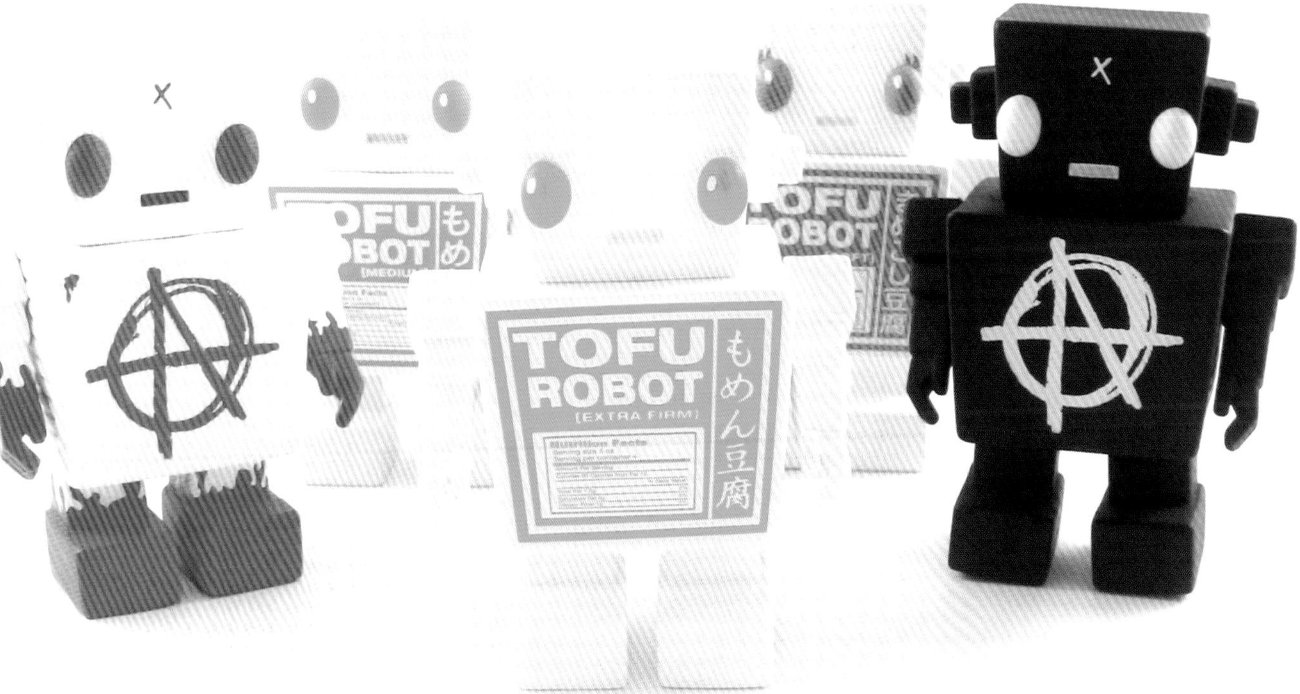
TOFU
ROBOT
[EXTRA FIRM]
もめん豆腐
Nutrition Facts

What's The Skinny

Clients and projects you last worked on?

I guess we're the client always trying to be fair to our designers.

Is there a message in your work or an issue that you want or try to address?

Our message is really up to the viewer. If you see something deep about it, great! If it makes you smile and brightens your day, even better!

What do you enjoy about your work.?

I love watching people's reactions to the designs. Most people have a big smile and their eyes light up with excitement when they see our stuff. But it's also funny to see people's reaction to our Sushi Neko line of characters. Sometimes they think we're advocating eating cats like sushi, which couldn't be further from the truth. Kazuko, the Sushi Neko designer, is the biggest lover of cats so I'm pretty sure that's not what she had in mind.

Where do you find insparation?

Food, mostly Japanese.

寿司猫
Sushi Neko

とうふ
mi so HOT

桜
kokeshi ink.

Mi So Happy
とうふ

Tim Tsui

Tim is one of the hottest Hong Kong illustrators and figure designers, actively participating in cross-discipline creative projects, locally and worldwide.

"Da TeamBronx" his own brand name, has been showcased around the globe, and his work sought out by big brand names such as Adidas and MTV.

Recently Tim added a new level of eccentricity and lavishness to his traditional figure design by applying real diamonds into his toys. This is an unique and pioneering idea which has earned him applause in Asia and the rest of the world.

"Visual communication is about spreading your ideas through art, burning bridges that other media find hard to surpass. Graffiti is a good example of this."

DA
GREY
017"

D5

DAPE
D5

020"

What's The Skinny

Clients and projects you last worked on?

The latest collaboration I was involved with was Coca-Cola and the 2008 Olympic Games. The project was producing a set of pins to be promoted during the games.

I'm proud that I was part of a project like this.

Is there a message in your work or an issue that you want or try to address?

My works are always looking at anger and ferocity, using these qualities to fight for dreams and respect.
I believe that everyone should have some dreams they should fight for. I like fashion very much, so I will combine some fashion trend with each of my designs.

What do you enjoy about your work?

I can do anything I want, I can go to many different countries to exhibit, and show people my work. Fans of my designs often e-mail me to let me know that they have one of my characters, this i enjoy very much.

Where do you find your inspiration?

I always get my ideas and inspiration from watching movies.

In 2004, Tim was invited to exhibit in a toy show organized by famous French fashion shop, Colette, and he was also asked to be the guest speaker at the Toyzworld Exhibition event.

In 2008 Tim began a world tour stopping in the USA, United Kingdom, France and other Asian countries.

Tim has been involved in projects with Coca-Cola, Royal Elastics, Tower Records, Colette and WAD Magazine.

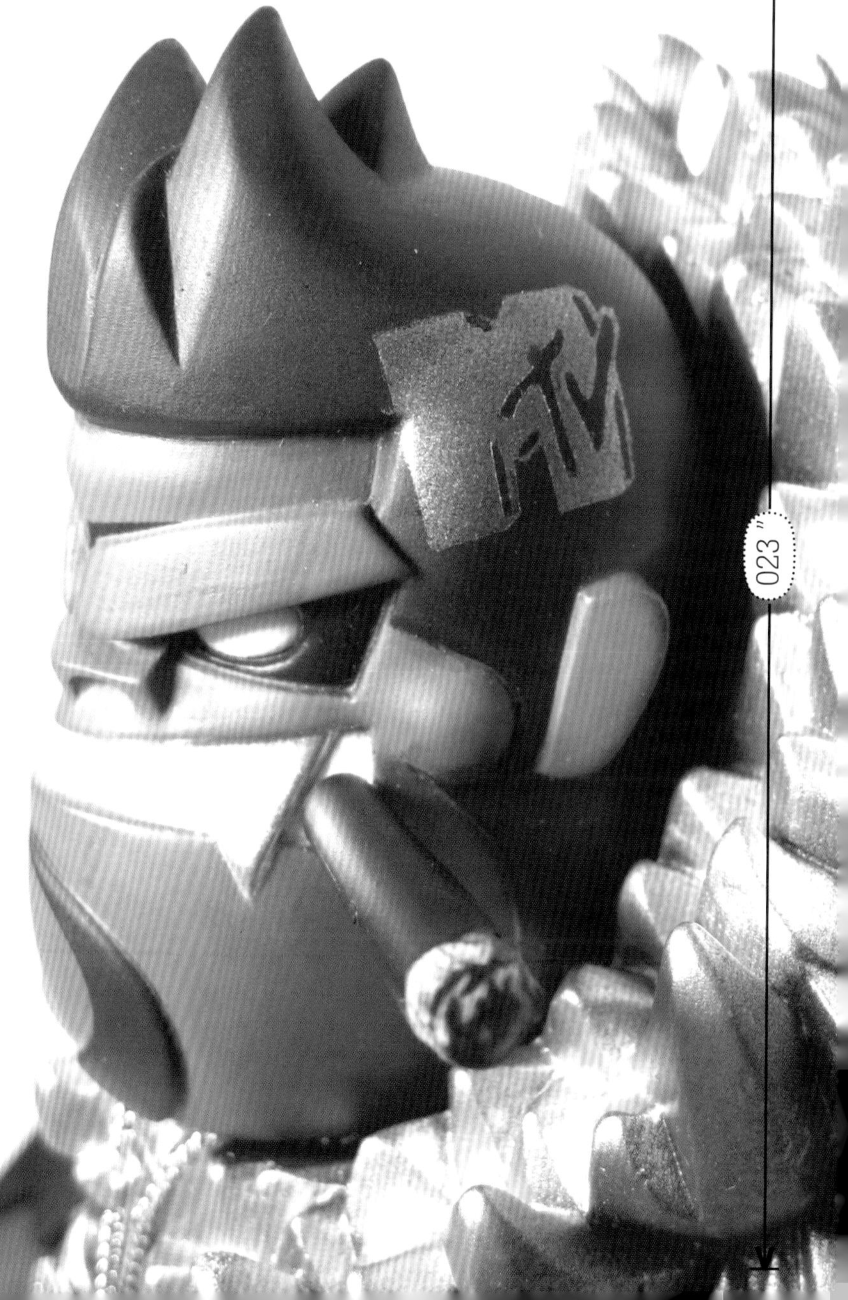

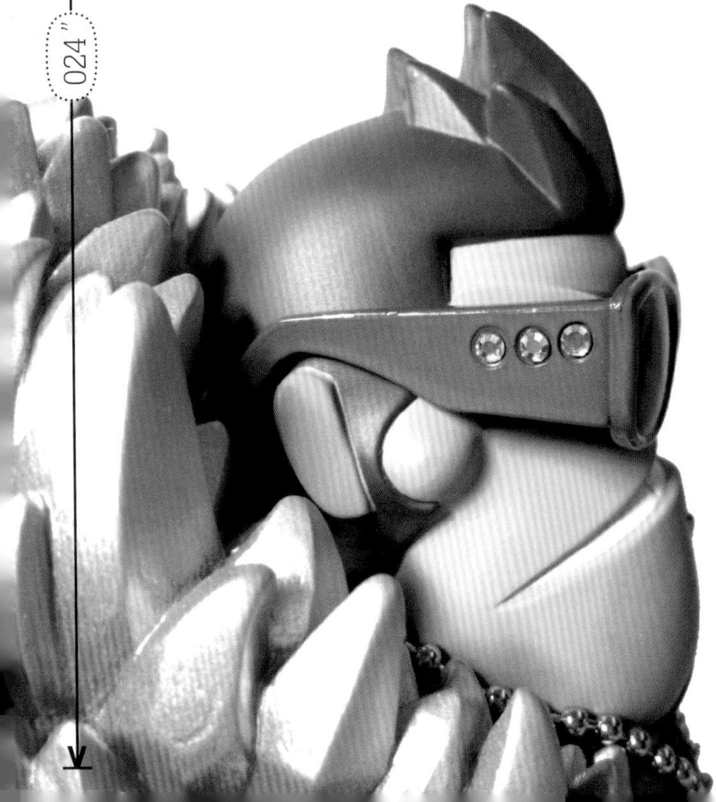

DA
TEAM

D1

dateambronx
"PLEASE DON'T SHAKE AND GET READY FOR IT"
WARNING:
Choking Hazard. Small parts.
Not for children under 10 years.
GRAY

01

01

teambronx
ASE DON'T SHAKE AND GET READY FOR IT"

DA

DA

WAD

DAPE

DAPE
D5

GOOD
VOTE
VOTE

Dacosta Bayley

Originally from Barbados in the Caribbean, Dacosta currently lives and works on the West Coast of Canada. He has been in the arts as long as he can remember; it's simply something he has always done. "From the time I could hold a crayon, there isn't a time when I can remember not wanting to create things or tell a story." Dacosta's preferred tool is digital media. So much so that he is trying to push his studio to an all-digital working environment.

Dacosta explores topics or things that interest him. He takes one idea and transplants it, or twists the context, mixing it up with futuristic forms and... just see what happens!

"I think the common theme that runs throughout all of my personal work is that of hope and optimism. I try to always communicate a story with my work. It's more satisfying to me when a character has a well thought out world to live in."

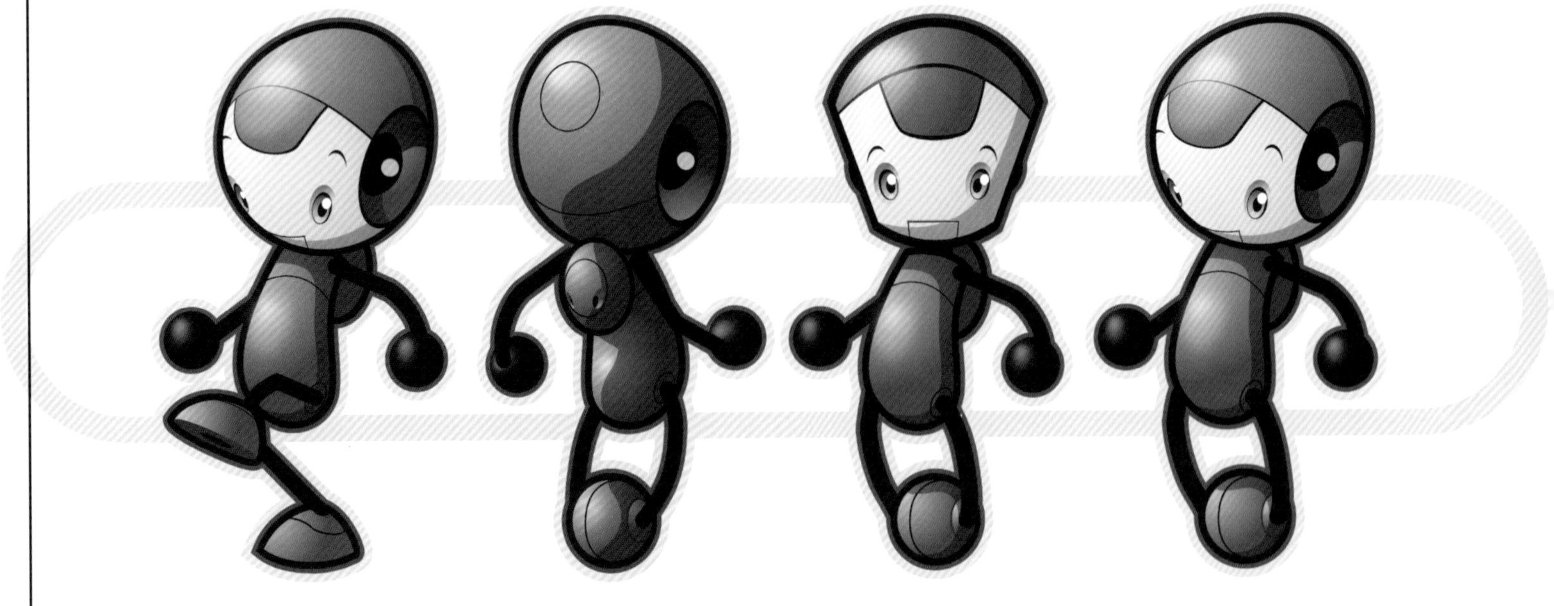

CHOCOLATE SOOP™

design creative

036"

What's The Skinny

Clients and projects you last worked on?

My client projects have been mainly focused around mascots and brand development.

Is there a message in your work or an issue that you want or try to address?

I believe my work speaks to a world of purpose. I want to create works that ask the viewer to look at themselves and the connection to the world around them.

What do you enjoy about your work?

The process is first. I design what I like. It's most important that out of the process, the end result is something that is an honest, unformulated expression of my imagination. If that expression results in other people enjoying the piece and wanting to add the work to their collection, then that makes it all the more rewarding.

Where do you find your inspiration?

I find inspiration in the possibilities of everyday living. Inspiration can come from the most unexpected places. I try to stay open to new ideas that may present themselves in whatever I happen to be working on, or wherever I happen to be.

ディクト
DCTO
jibun project
www.dctoproject.com

Red: Overall Good Luck Energy

Yellow: Safe Journey

Black: Strong Profits

Pink: Love and Good Birth

Purple: Long, Safe Life

Blue: Self-development

Green: Good Health

White: Celebrations and Academic

Gold: Money and Improve Life

Silver: Push out Bad Luck

DCTO_Chibi Charms

禅

"Once I get that spark I ask myself, 'What is it about this thing or idea that I find appealing?' In the research phase I look for elements which I feel can develop into a story or that will help grow the concept that is being hinted at. When there seems to be enough inspirational material to play with, I start piecing it all together to build a story around my initial spark. As the project starts to take shape, inevitably opportunities to expand, or deepen the concept pop-up. It's very important that each element balances with the piece as a whole. The form naturally dictates the "rules" of what it wants to be, what works and what doesn't. Whether I'm creating a character, designing packaging, or promotional material, I simply push it along until it feels complete."

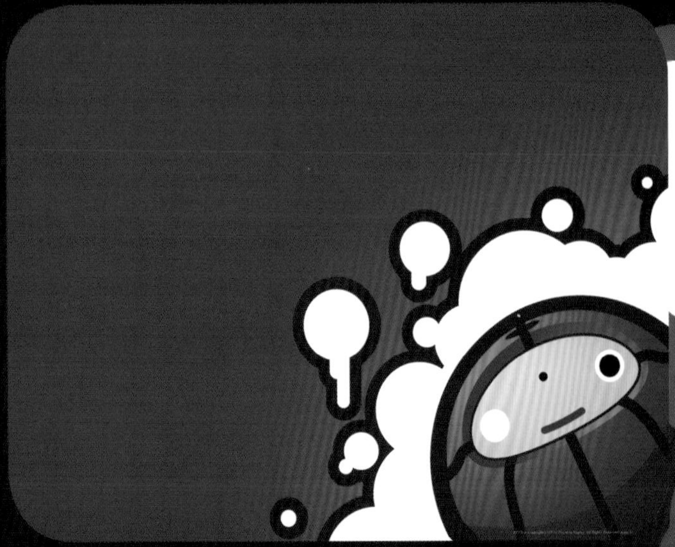

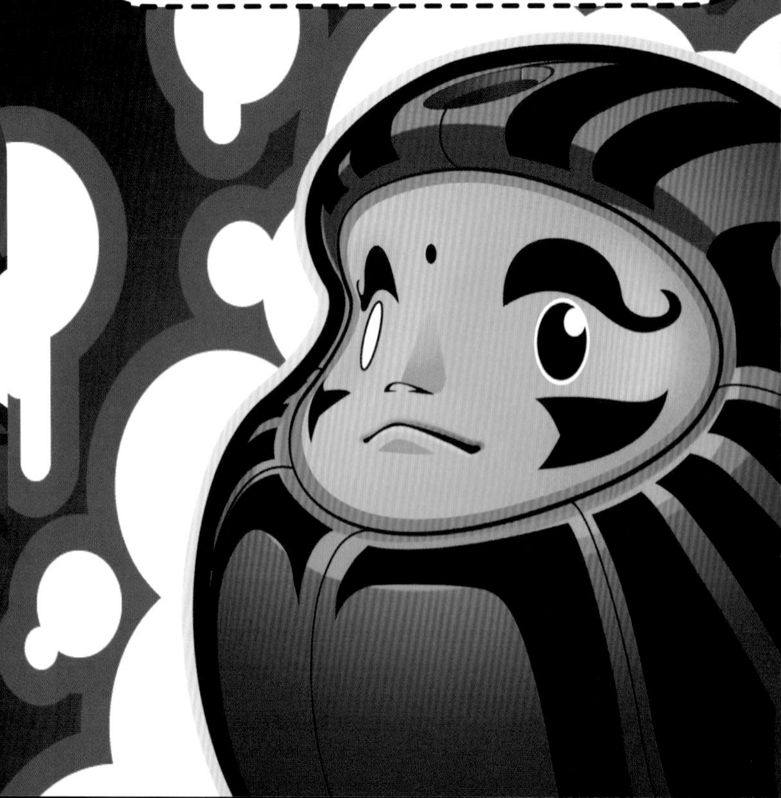

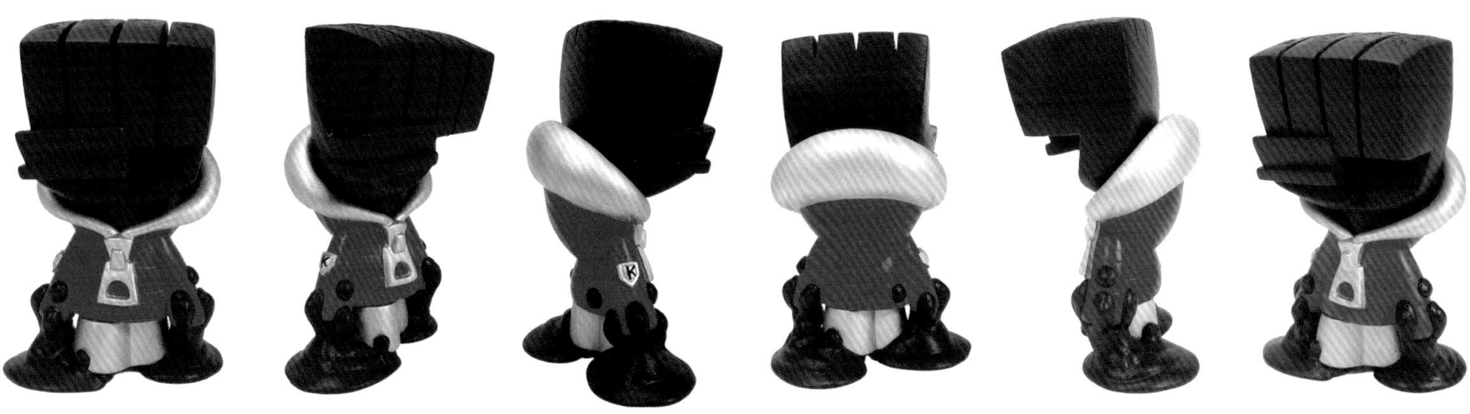

COLD
HOT

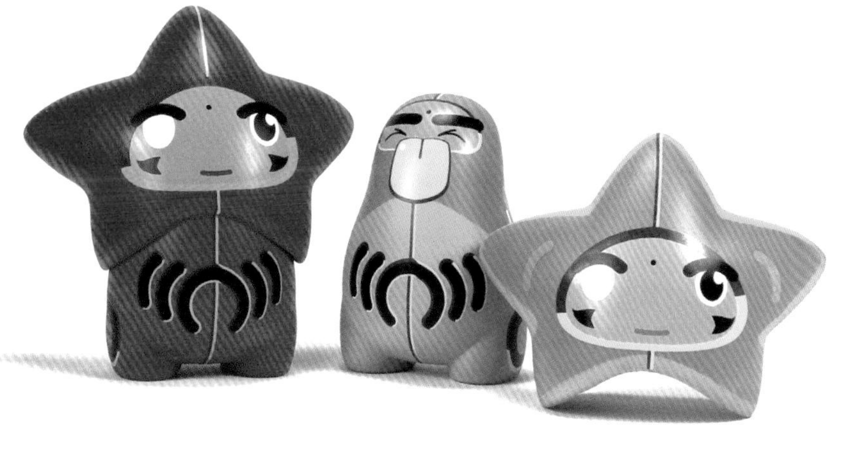

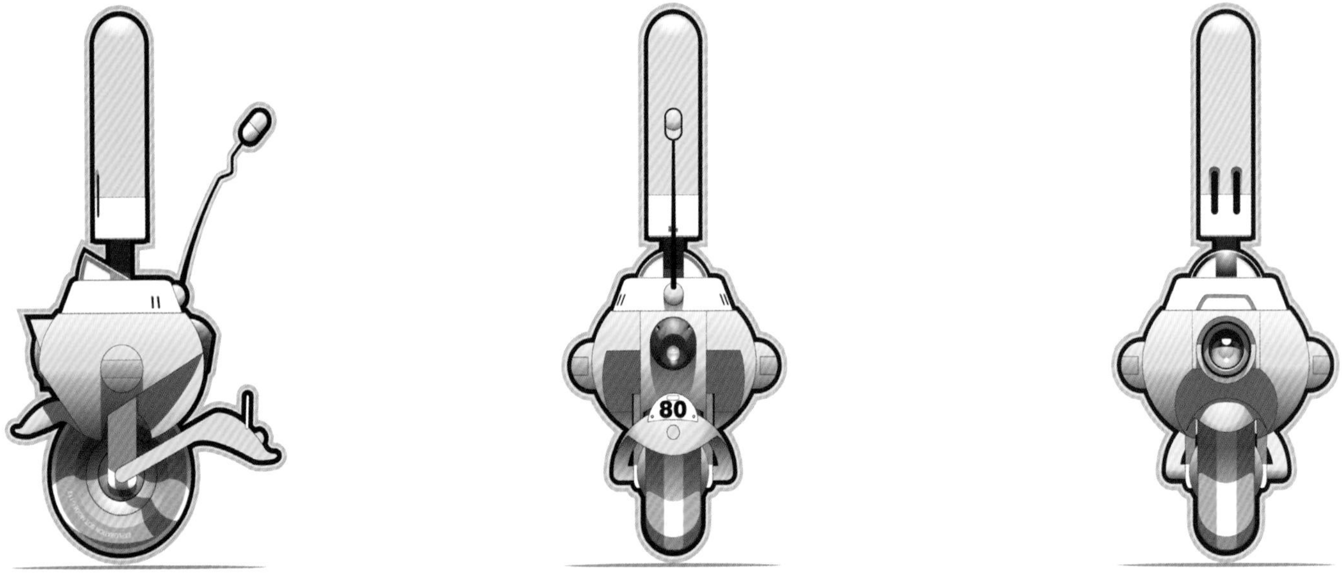

Left Rear Front

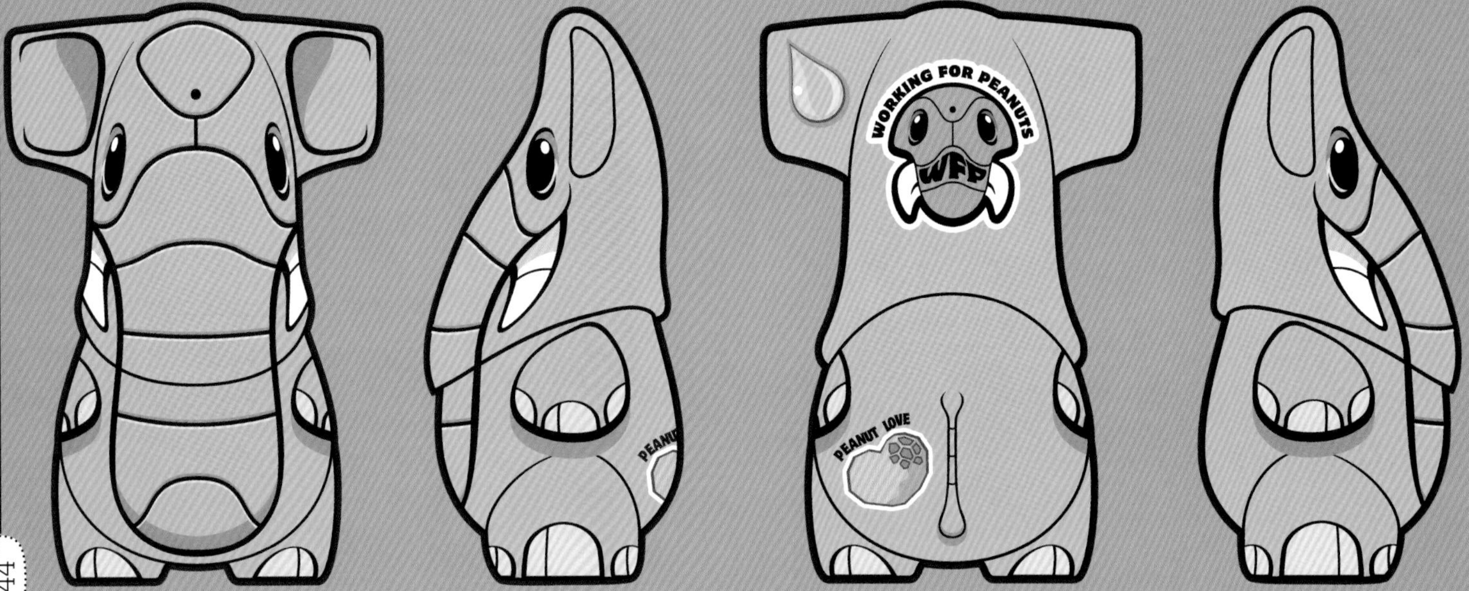

Working for Peanuts
by Dacosta

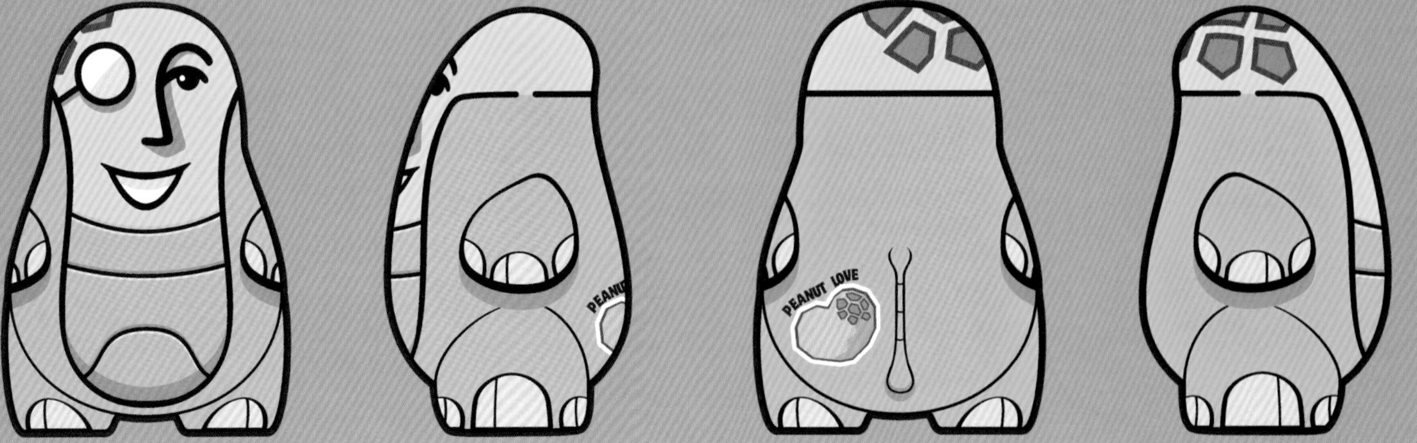

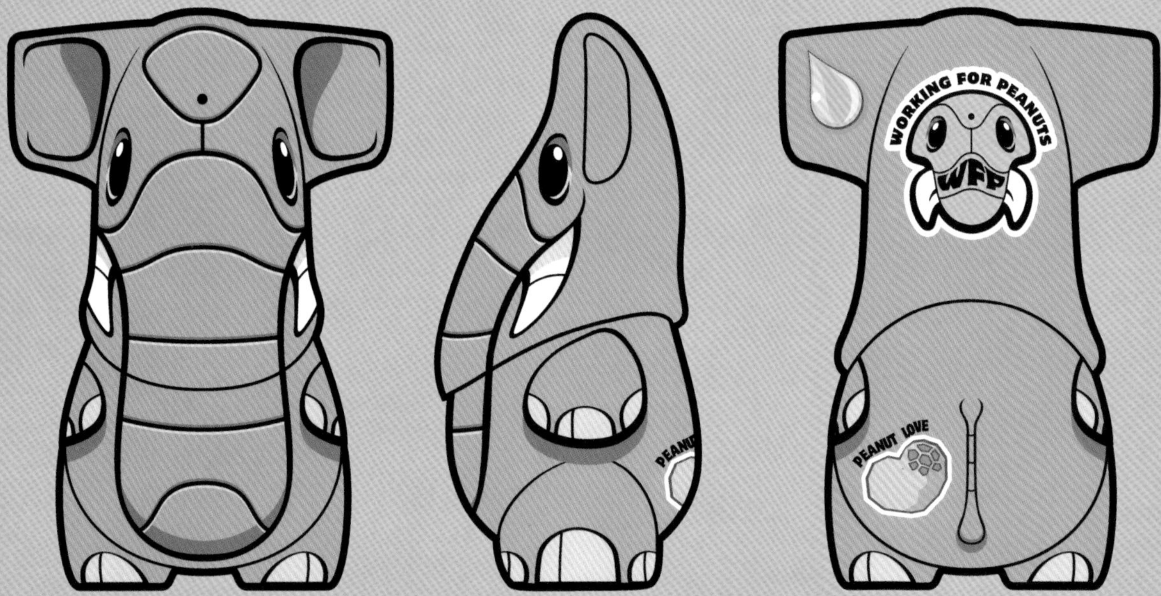

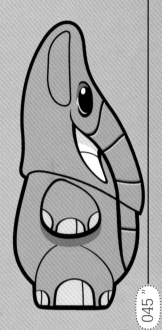

Working for Peanuts

by Dacosta

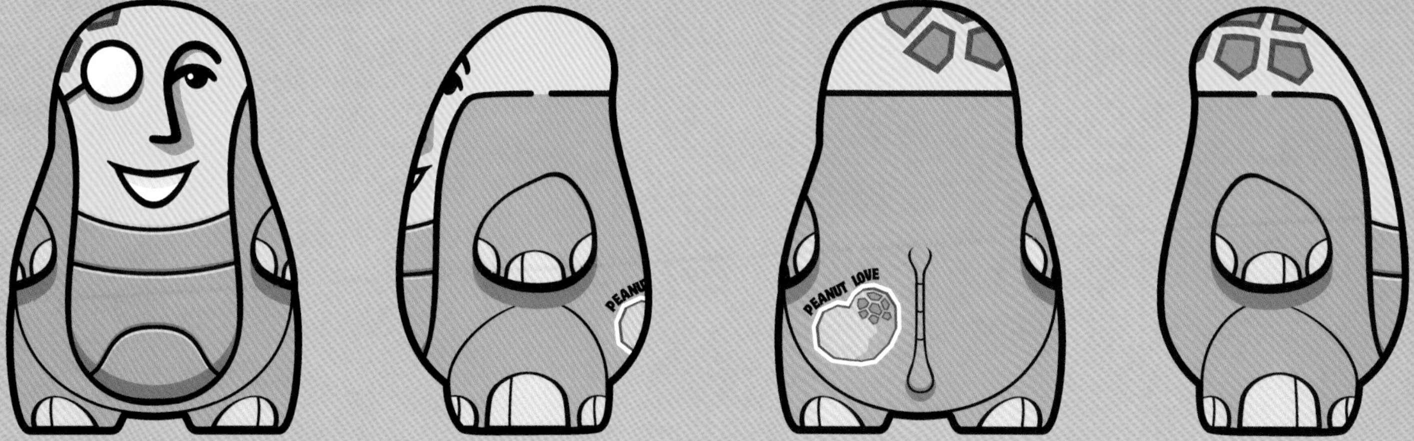

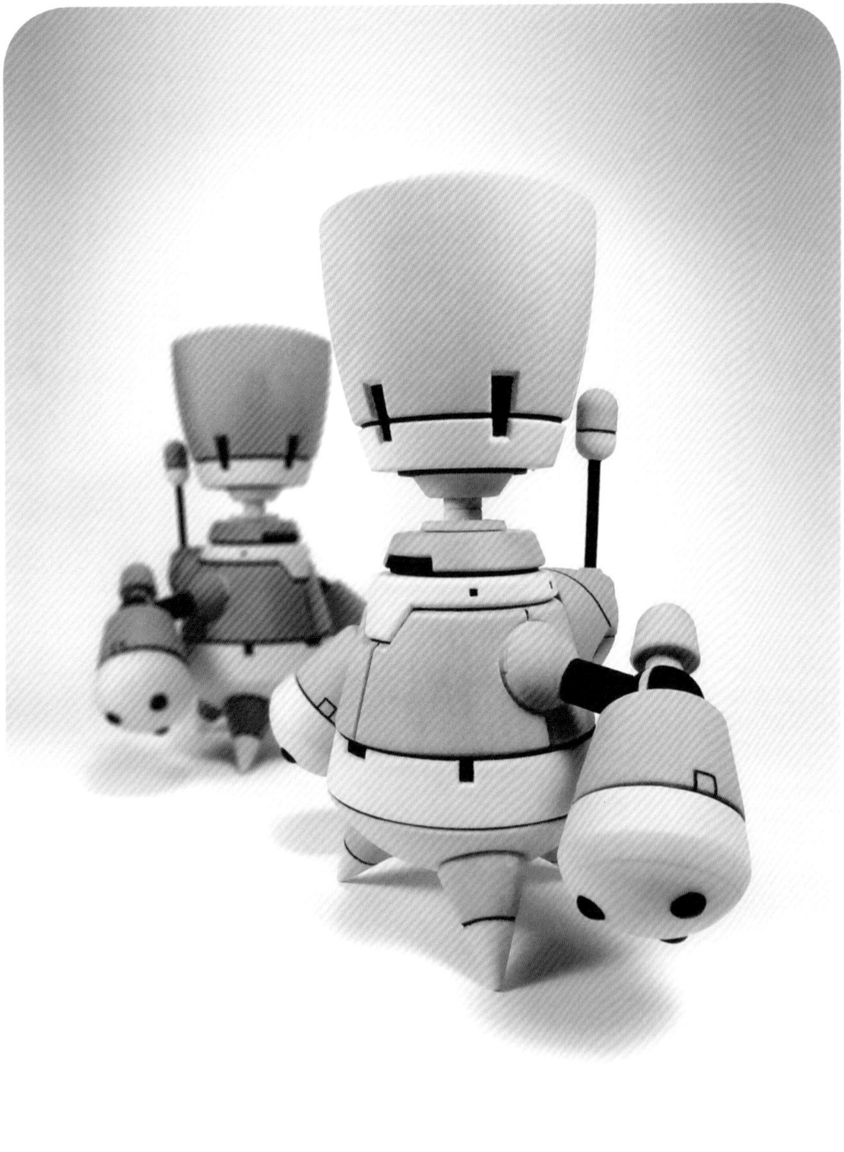

CONDENSED
DARK CHOCOLATE

Riot68

Out of Nottingham, England, this artist's preferred media is 'walls'. This is so, because of his love for large scale graffiti murals. He has been in and around art since childhood, and inspiration for his works comes from all around him, sometimes consciously, other times unconsciously.
Concepts start off as a doodle in his sketchbook and end up as full blown ideas, but throughout it all, Riot68 tells us that "...freedom of expression and fun is the key to all my works".

"Be sure to keep your eye on riot68.com and thanks to all my friends and my family for their support, especially my extraordinary wife..."

66
10

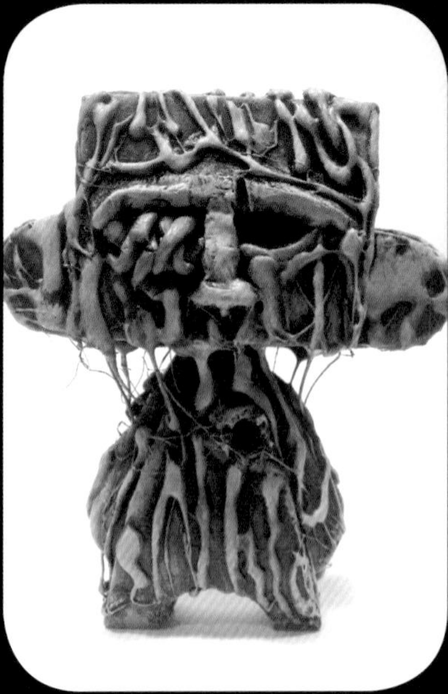

What's The Skinny

Clients and projects you last worked on?

I work a lot with young people and on community projects, helping young people express themselves through art and take pride in what they do. I do this not only with sketching and graffiti but with video projects and other digital art forms.

Is there a message in your work or an issue that you want or try to address?

I like to look at human traits and also explore the darker side of human existence. Lots of my work is inspired by the kids I work with.

What do you enjoy about your work?

All of it. My wife once said that if I was unemployed I'd be doing exactly the same things as I do for a job, and I can't argue with that. It's great to see the community reacting to projects I have worked on with them and the local young people.

Where do you find your inspiration?

From everything; mostly the people in my life.

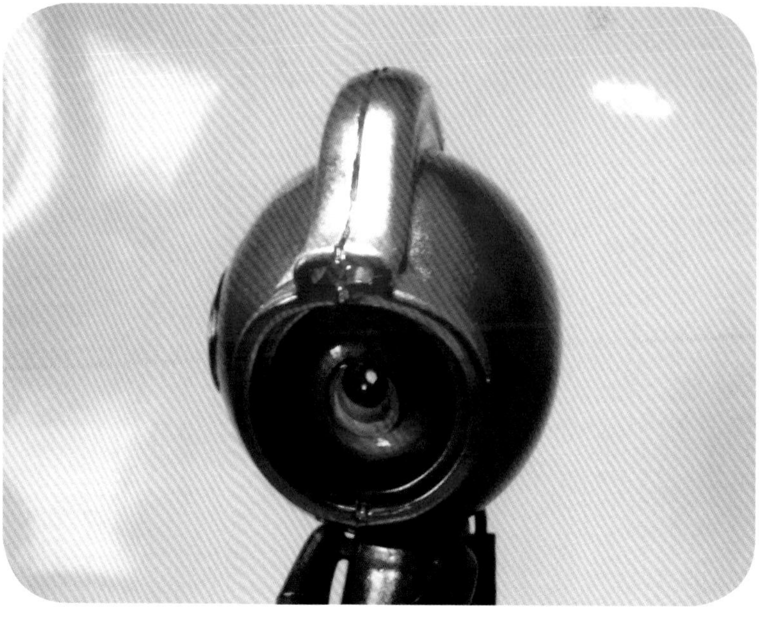

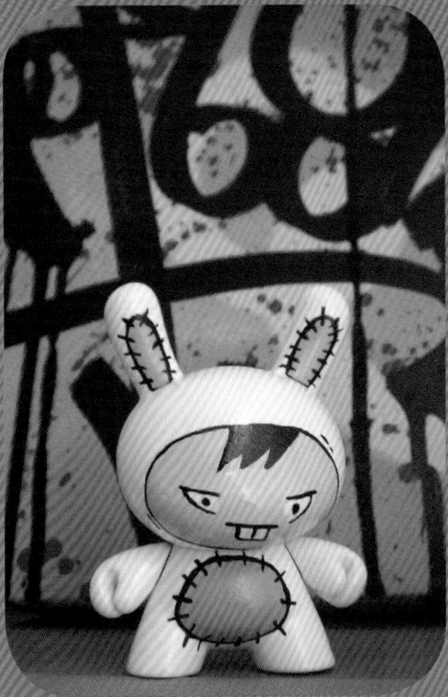

Riot80

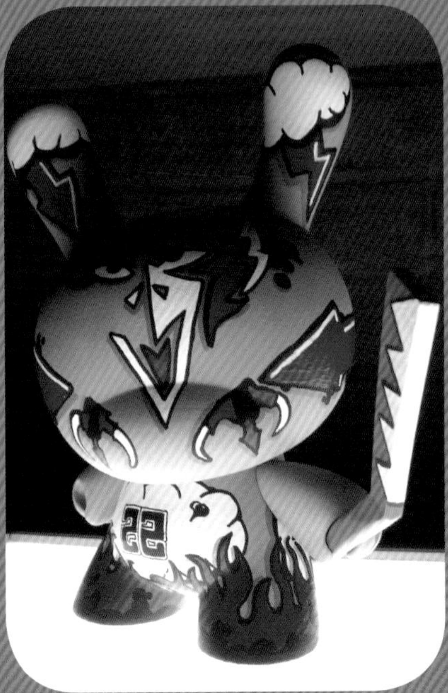

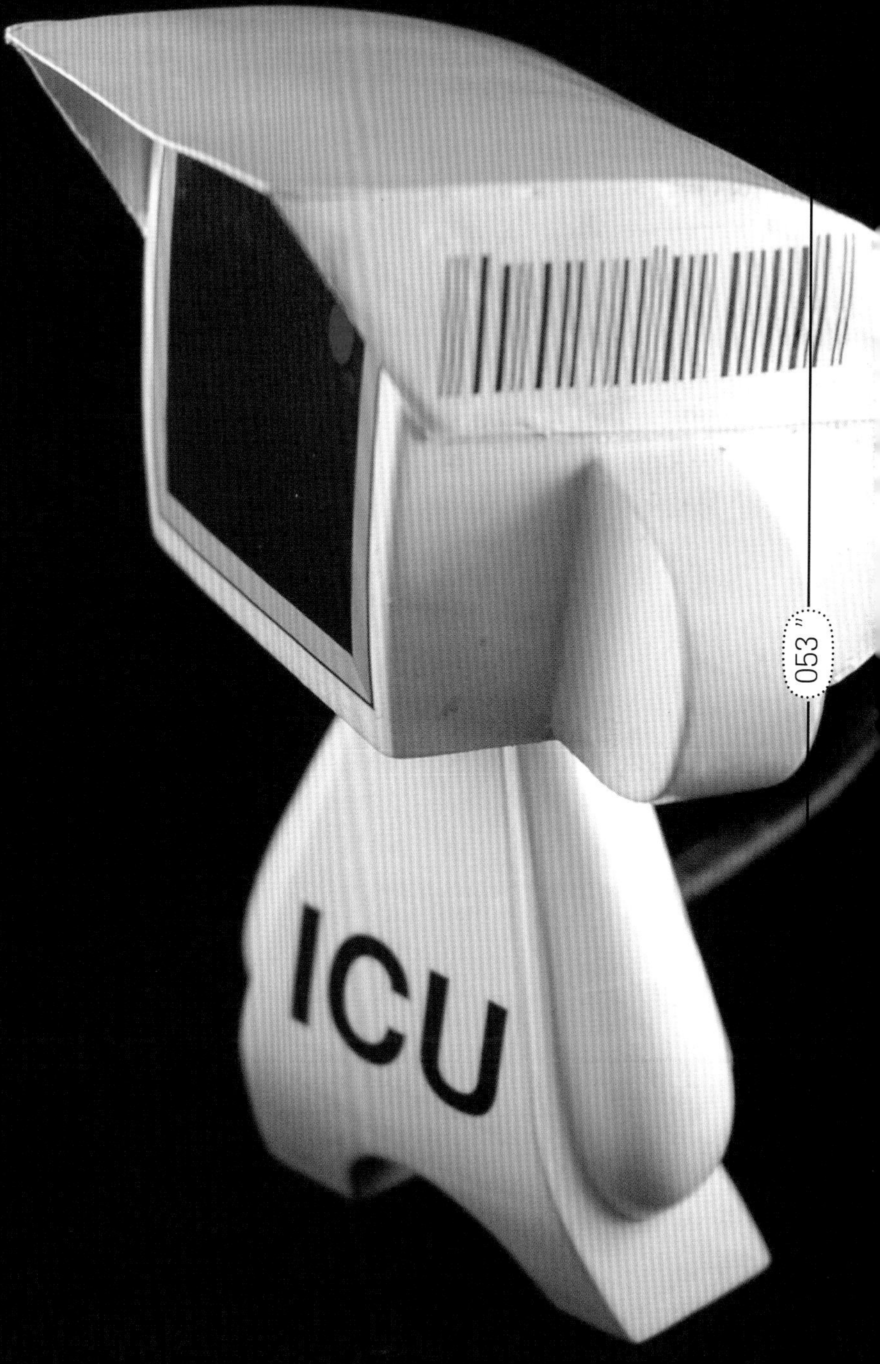
ICU

68

68

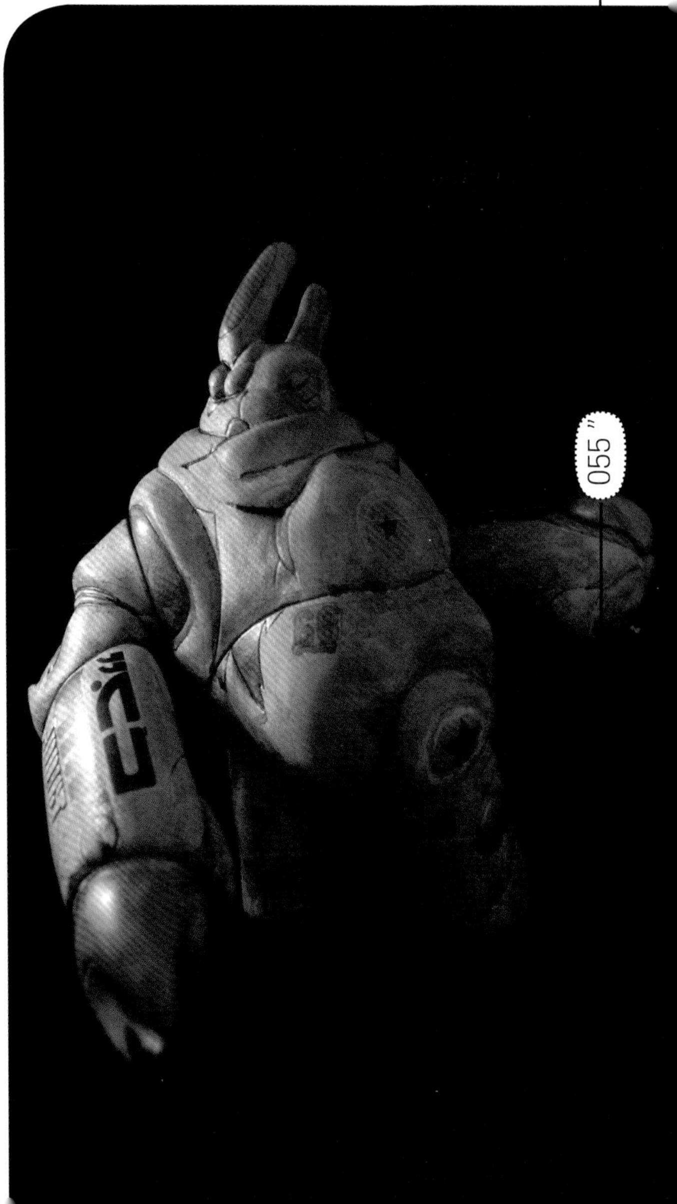

Chapman Tse

From Hong Kong, China, Chapman has been working for 10 years and combines animation with graphic design to create something fun and easy to be understood, by the mass audience.

"Good old pencil and paper" together with digital applications and fiberglass, are his usual preferred media.

He gets his inspiration from idle sketching and the different books he reads, whilst endeavouring to break into public art (one of his favorite mediums being sculpture).

"It's time to blur the boundary between visual communication and visual art, to make it more inspiring and meaningful, and this is what I'm trying to do in the recent years and the future."

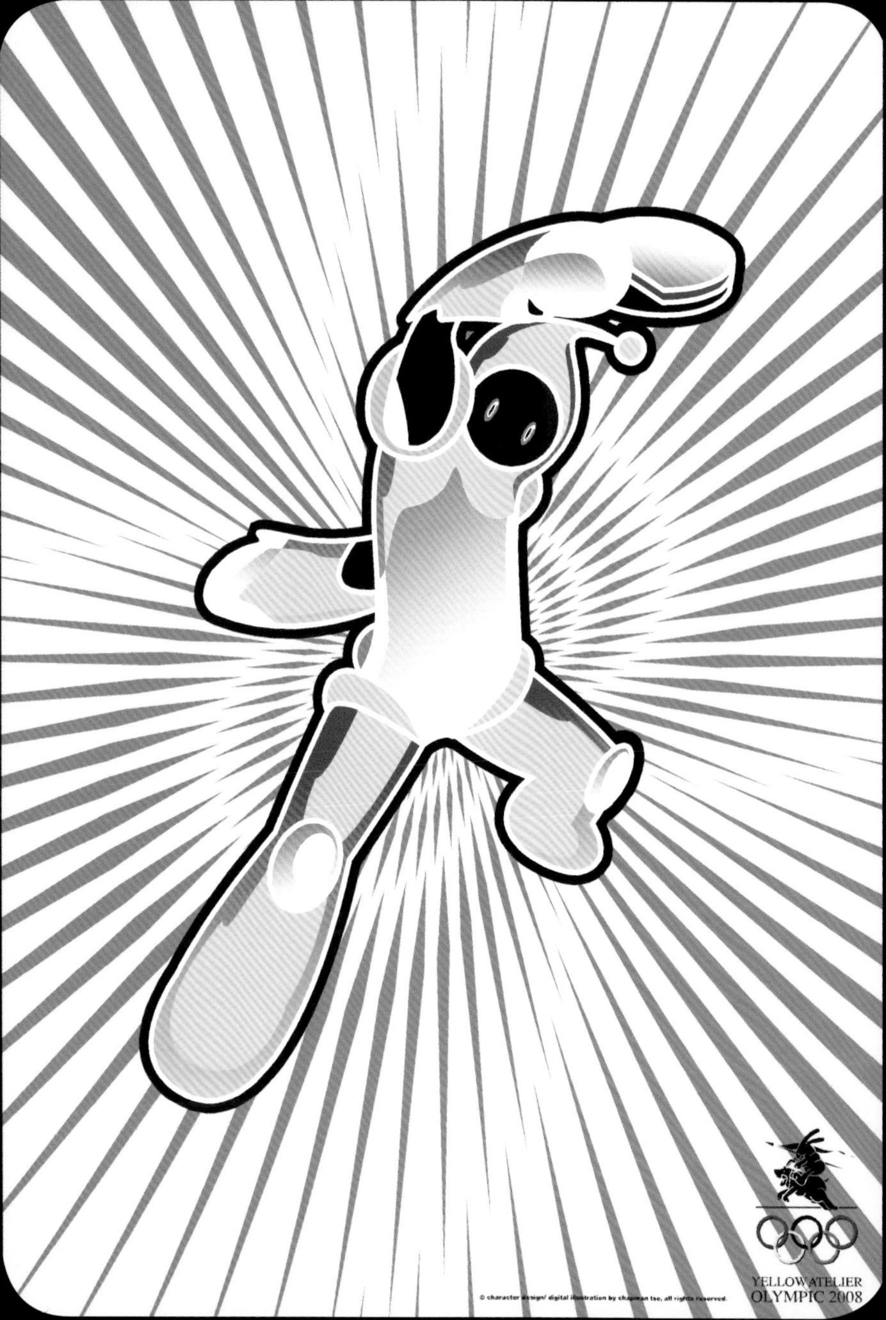
YELLOW ATELIER
OLYMPIC 2008

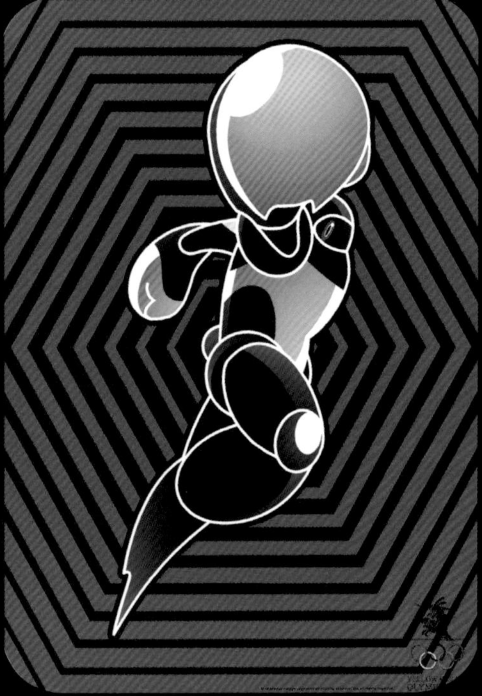

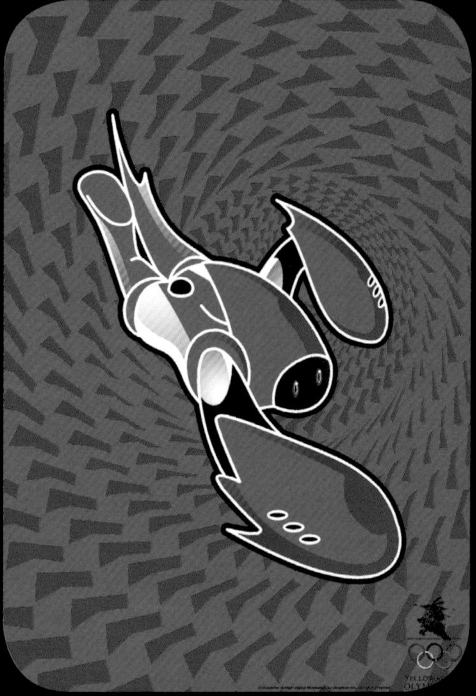

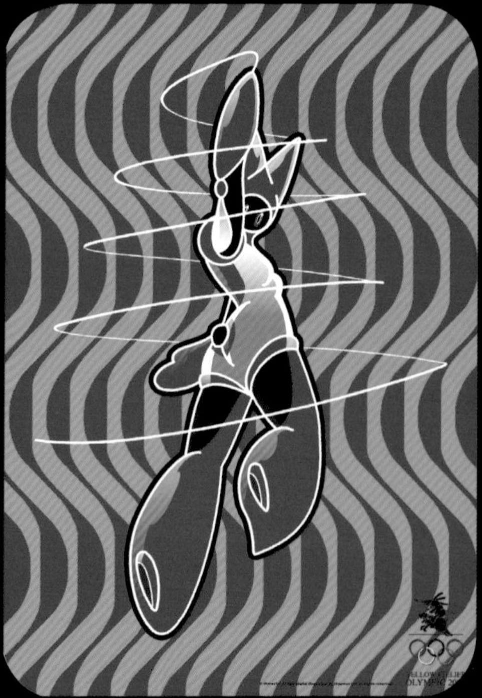

What's The Skinny

Clients and projects you last worked on?

Graphics, packaging, web sites and branding design.

Is there a message in your work or an issue that you want or try to address?

To seek your own identity and self value, to live a colorful life.

What do you enjoy about your work?

The process, people's reaction and self review of my works.

Where do you find your inspiration?

Comics, animation, newspapers and our surrounding world.

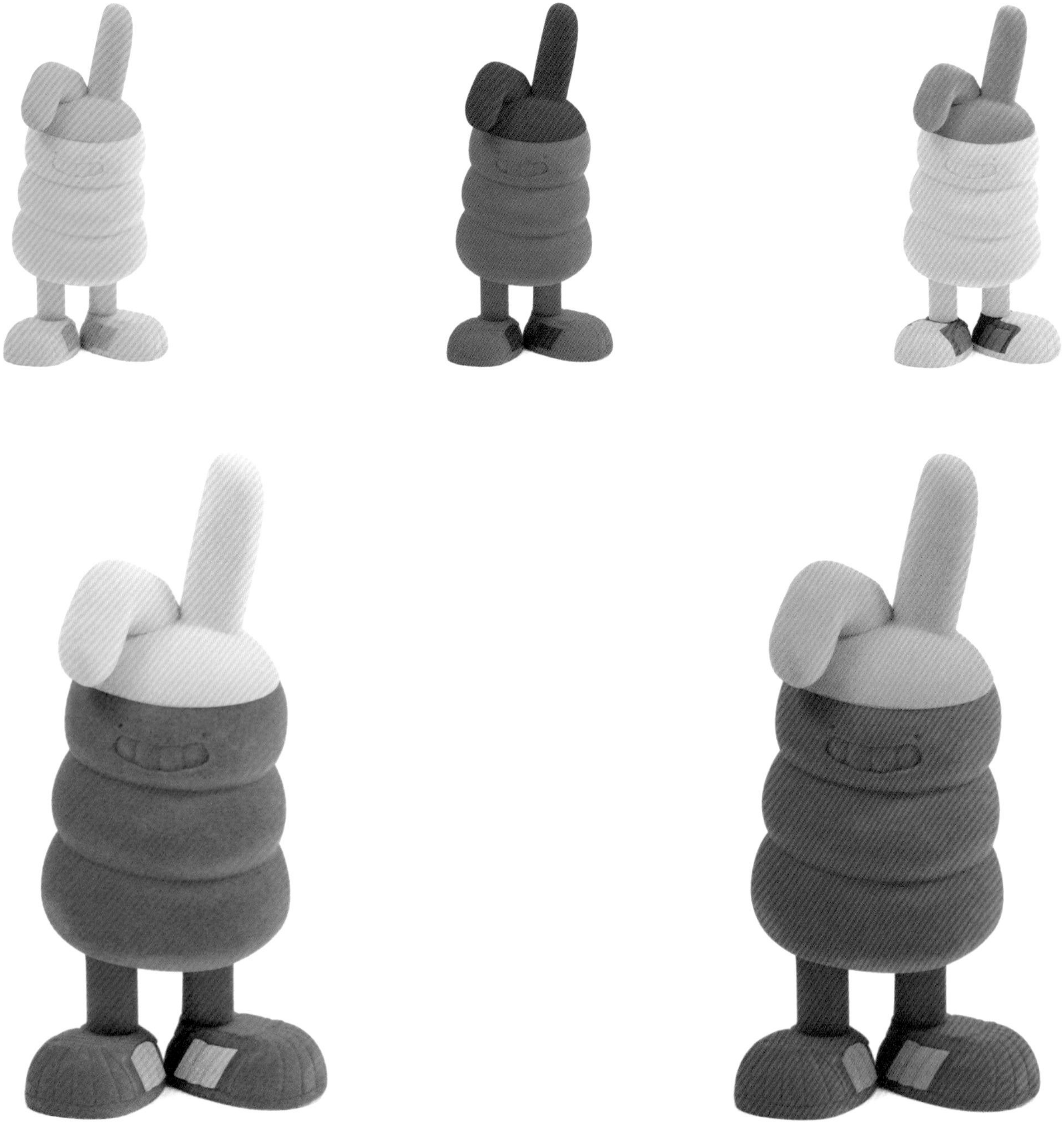

YELLOW
ATELIER.
I ♥ YELLOW
I ♥ YELLO
YELLOW
ATELIER.
190"

Hicalorie

Established by Alex Devol way back when; it is known by some as a collective of artists, by others as a brand, maybe a graffiti tag, a skate team, a clothing line or sometimes just a bunch of odd-but-likable people.

Design outfit Hicalorie is built on a love for collaboration, cake, colours and creating things. Hicalorie Has independently produced this & that, from skateboards and sneakers to T-shirts and toys, while also hosting and participating in art exhibits and group shows around the globe.

Determined to splash itself over every corner of the design spectrum, Hicalorie's artwork has also been featured on album sleeves, magazine covers, art books, sneakers, clothing, animations, painted canvases, and toys.

"The best part is the excitement I have just before starting something new and the satisfaction I get when it's all finished and I can move onto something else".

063"
Hicalorie

hugs not

Lefty
Hicalorie
Hugs not drugs

What's The Skinny

Clients and projects you last worked on?

Recently I've been concentrating on Hicalorie's clothing line and its sudden growth. Adfunture Workshops have given me the chance to try my mouse at creating some vinyl toys. I've had a lot of fun doing some artist-collaborations with Julie West, DGPH, Superdeux and others.

What do you enjoy about your work?

The finished product mostly. I have a great time working on projects but generally the best part is the excitement I have just before starting something new and the satisfaction I get when it's all finished and I can move onto something else.

Where do you find your inspiration?

Everywhere really; old movies, music, comic books, the internet, people and day-to-day stuff. Music's important though, I rarely draw without a song playing and it often affects the result.

HICALORIE
Hicalorie

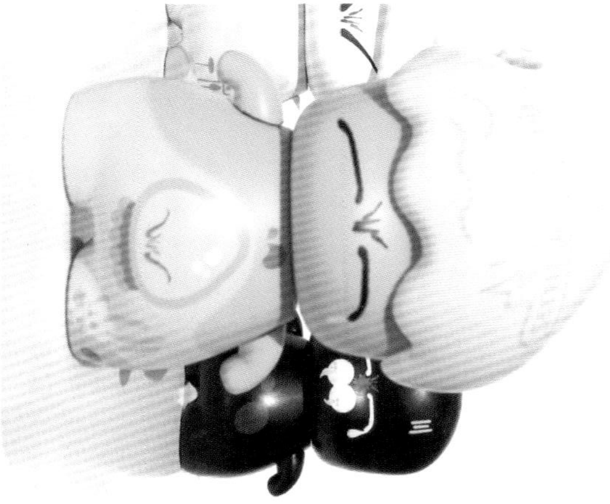

Jesse Hernandez

Well known for his "Urban Aztec" or "Urban Native" style, a fusion of indigenous culture with urban street style, this "Califaztlan" tries to make art that will stand the test of time, both in style and relevance.

A varied artist in his used media, he can go through vinyl, paints, marker, airbrush, digital and of course, "the almighty pencil" to create his works.

When it comes to his methods he is pretty straight forward, "concept, sketch, attack!"

Although drawing since he was a kid, Hernandez has been in the fine arts and design fields working seriously for 11 years, but his motto still stands the same at "Put some soul in your work."

"I hope that the voice of the native or indigenous tribes of the Americas is heard through all of my artistic visions."

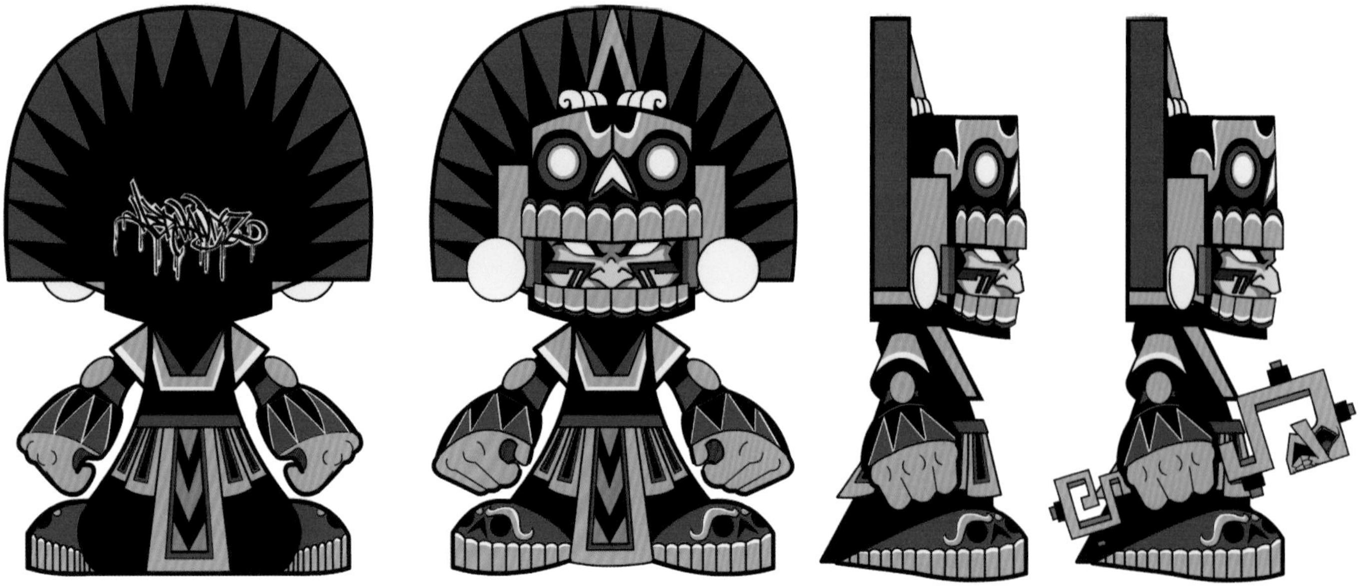

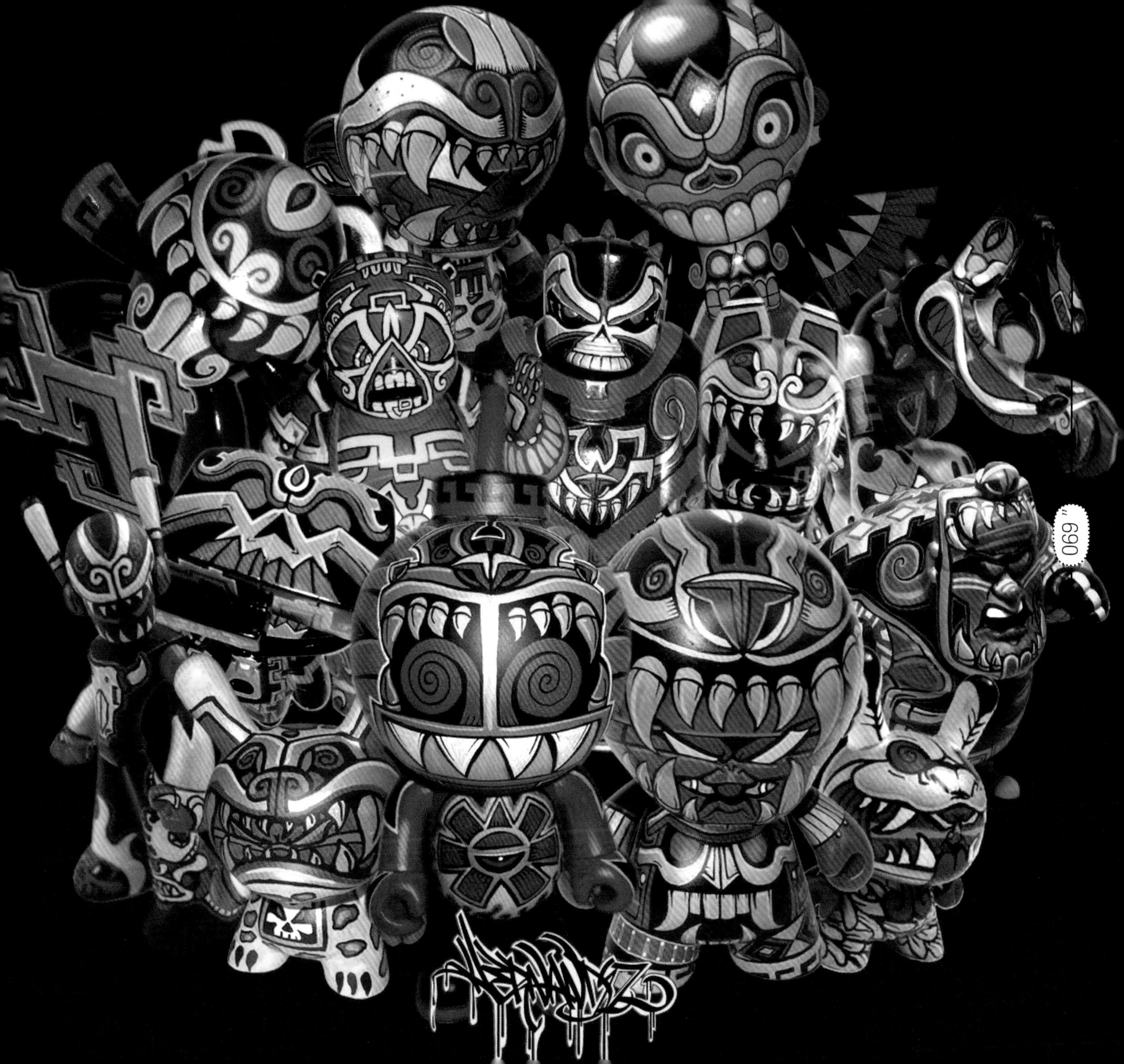

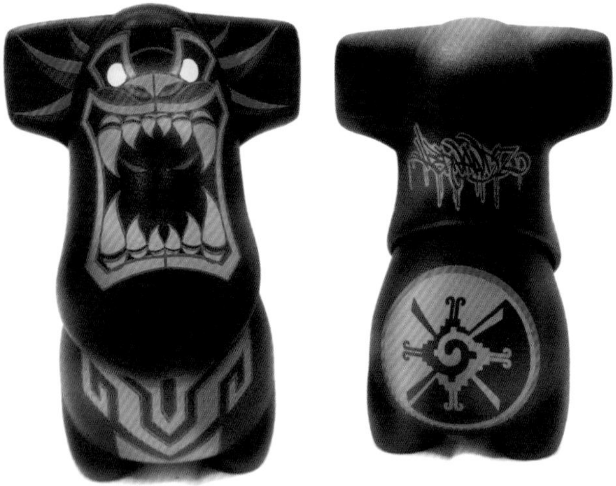

What's The Skinny

Clients and projects you last worked on?

I am currently working as the Art Director/co-creator of the cartoon "The Nutshack" for The Filipino Channel (www.thenutshack.net). I am also putting out some new original toys with Super Rad Toys, ToyQube, Kaching Brands and some other companies as well. I've also been doing gallery shows all over the place.

Is there a message in your work or an issue that you want or try to address?

My work has many sides to it, and the message can change with each piece. Everyone draws out something different from my work. However I hope that the voice of the native or indigenous tribes of the Americas is heard through all of my artistic visions, and can inspire other people and artists alike.

What do you enjoy about your work?

I love seeing people's reactions, I put myself through a very difficult process. Like many other artists, I can be my toughest critic, but it's always worth it when I hear people's reactions.

Where do you find your inspiration?

I'm very inspired by Ancient Culture, Graffiti, Cartoonz, Comics, Vinyl Toyz, Music, and other artists.

© JESSE HERNANDEZ 2007

Mad-l (MOD l) n. A representative style, plan, or design

MINIS

FRONT R. SIDE BACK

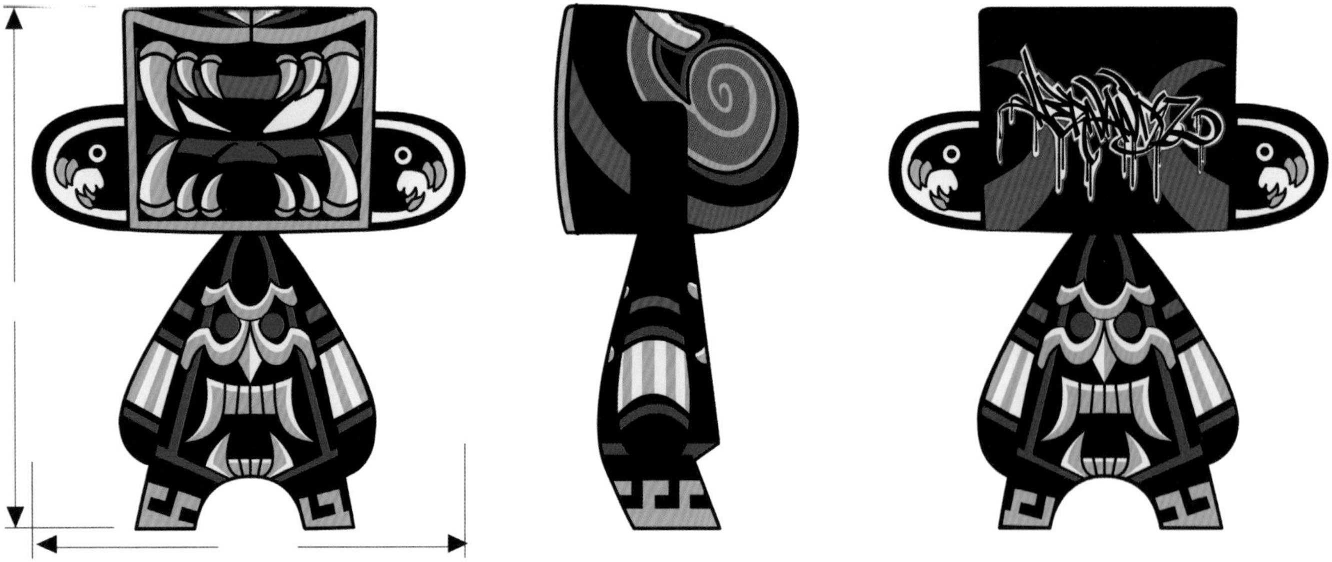

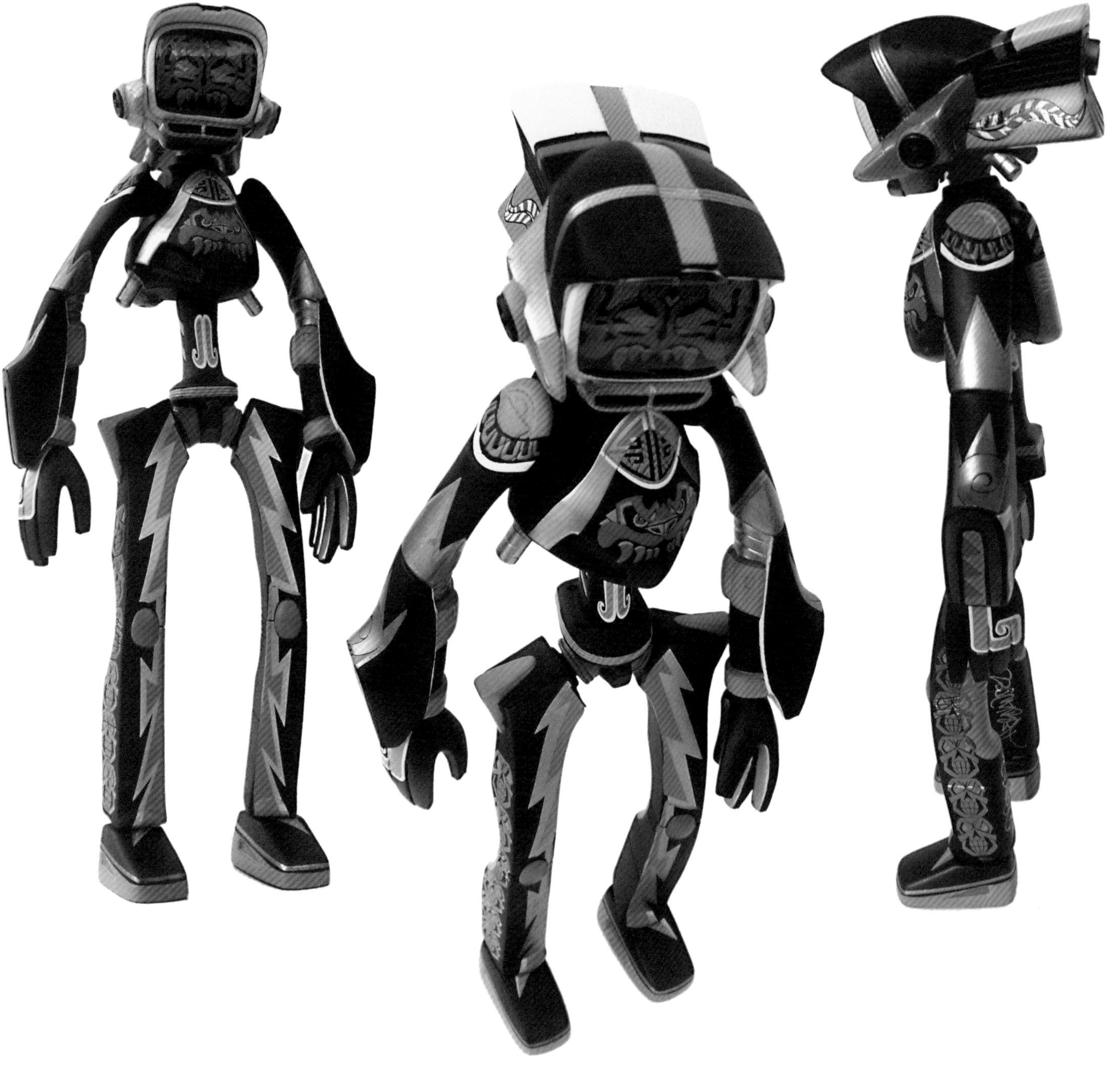

"Ozomatli" the Aztec Monkey
By :Jesse Hernandez
All rights Reserved 2007
w.immortalstudios.net

18"

GOT NUTZ
DICKMAN
BIG DAWG

THE NUTSHACK
NUTZ

BEEYOTCH

REMO

Charuca

Charuca from Barcelona, Spain, comes across as a sweet, relaxed and life-loving person. All this reflects in her work which, mainly aimed at girls and children, has most of her characters sharing the same traits: being cute and sweet (she specializes in Kawaii and cute designs). Charuca also has a very practical side to her work, so all her characters also have an application in the real world as lifestyle products.

This 33 year-old designer gives us an insight on how she develops her work; "After the idea, I do the draft in a piece of paper. When it's like I want, I scan it and then I apply the colors using my computer. I do the vector with flash or freehand. Sometimes I apply some final touches using Photoshop."

"I try to make people laugh. In my world there's no pain"

charuca.net
ちゃるーか
★ THE CHARACTERS FACTORY ★
WWW.CHARUCA.NET
hello
(again)
charuca@charuca.net

SUGAR KILLS
PANTONE 209U
PANTONE 304U
PANTONE 1767U
PANTONE 209U
092"
SUGAR KILLS
SUGAR KILLS
charuca
www.charuca.net

ちゃるーか

What's The Skinny

Clients and projects you last worked on?

All kind of projects always related to cute characters and merchandising applications. My favorite client is myself. When I have a chance I work on my own character line. My dream is to, in the future, find Charuca stuff everywhere. At the same time I create characters or concept art for brands all around the world.

Is there a message in your work or an issue that you want or try to address?

I try to make people laugh. In my world there's no pain. I try to make people forget their daily life problems and just enjoy themselves.

What do you enjoy about your work?

The best thing about my work is, I can dedicate all my time to the thing I like the most, the cute characters and kawaii culture. I enjoy everything. Creating characters, travelling to Japan looking for inspiration, dealing with the clients. I feel very lucky because I enjoy it all.

Where do you find your inspiration?

Japan is my main source. I love Tokyo, its people and culture. I feel like I have been a Japanese girl in a past life. The first time I went to Tokyo I fell in love. Now I'm just thinking of going back again and again! The characters are everywhere. I LOVE San-X, the very best character factory, and of course I also like Sanrio.

ちゃるーか
charuca
www.charuca.net

095"

960″

Strawberry

Pear

Orange

Skwat
wear different
The best tees & goodies Mac Addict Store
skwat.be
www.skwat.be

860"

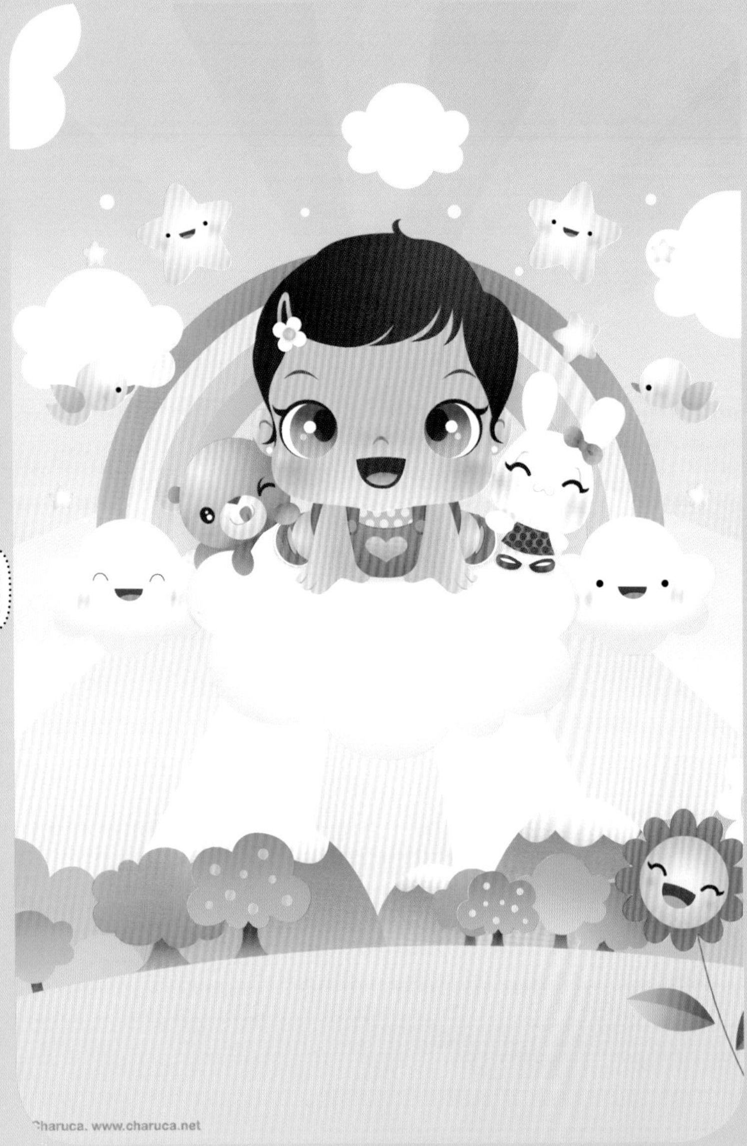

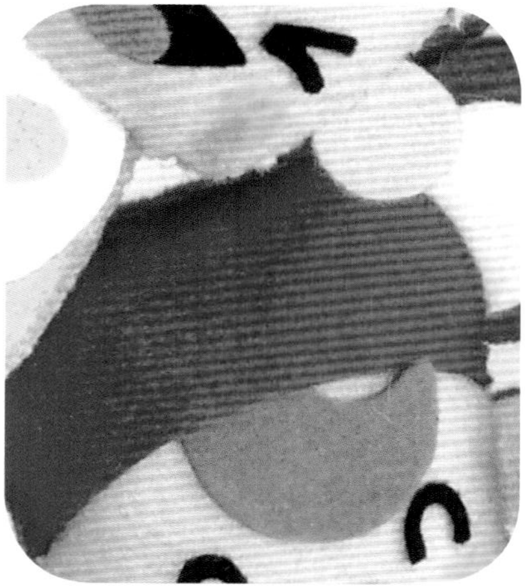
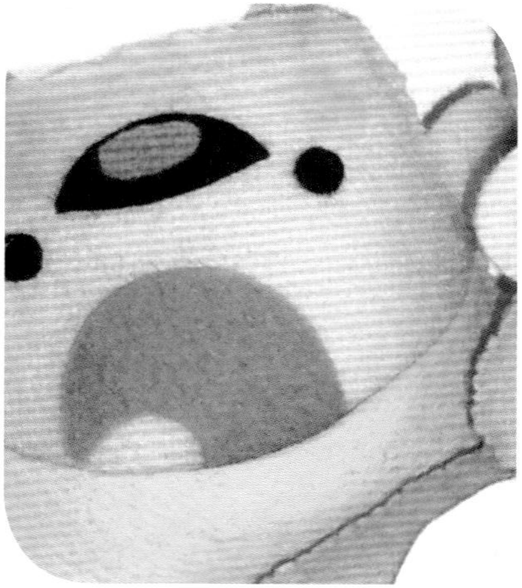

charuca
www.charuca.net

うどん
good&healthy
charuca
www.charuca.net
udon
JAPANESE FOOD.YUMMY!
UDON IS A TYPE OF THICK WHEAT-BASED NOODLE POPULAR IN JAPANESE CUISINE

102"

Kokechan
© Charuca. All rights reserved

UpPedete
Con su increíble sistema de propulsión a pedo!!!
charuca.net
Kokechan
© Charuca 2007. All rights reserved

OCTOPUS
www.charuca.net

charucashop
CUTE THINGS FOR KAWAII PRINCESS
www.charucanet/shop

Boo is removable!
Tinaboo®
&Boo
FRONT
BACK
Tinaboo®
&Boo

charuca

charuca

Alice Chan

After spending 9 years studying a variety of art and design subjects, nowadays, Alice Chan uses this background to call upon when creating something new.

For her, ideas can appear anytime and anywhere, even whilst "shopping, eating or travelling."

Alice Chan's clients are key global brands from all over the world, constantly drawing attention on this talented cross media illustrator and designer.
Her own brand "Asteria" carries a special meaning with it "… Asteria's eyelashes are 360 degrees, her eyes like a sparkling star. Stars stand for warmth, hope and good wishes."

"Everyone must have their dreams and wishes. I hope people that see my work will feel warm and happy and that their wishes will one day come true".

Qee®
Key Chain Collection
Patent No.HK1040350
TOY2R®
www.toy2r.com
www.asterialand.com
Alice Chen

ATLAS
FASHION ASTERIALAND
FOR COLETTE
BURBERRY PRORSUM / ALEXANDER MCQUEEN / CHLOÉ

SPORTMAX
x
alice chan
© Sportmax. All Rights Reserved.
© asteria / alice chan. limited edition
Sandra

108"

*** www.asterialand.com ***

SPORTMAX
SPORTMAX
X alice chan
" I really wanted to create something that would represent the different facets of modern women. I wanted to capture the carefree spirit of the young, dreamy girl in all of us."
get your
free gift

What's The Skinny

Clients and projects you last worked on?

Fendi, Levi's, Anna Sui, Goessele, Sportmax, Colette, Coca Cola, Sakamoto, Canon, MTV, Pictoplasma, Die Gestalten, Times Square Shopping Mall, Fashion and Beauty Magazine and Milk Magazine.

Is there a message in your work or an issue that you want or try to address?

I want my characters to bring out a positive message to the world. Asteria means a starry cut gemstone. I really hope my work can always encourage positive thinking.

What do you enjoy about your work?

Of course I enjoy the process of every project and art piece. My design and arts are popular and liked by many international clients and fans from over the world.

Where do you find your inspiration?

My favorite fairy tale is Alice in Wonderland. Because I loved it so much when I was a child, I used Alice as my English name. I also like Hans Christian Andersen. I got to illustrate the story "The Little Match Girl" in commemoration of his 200th birthday in 2005.

1/10
pen
SOGO
HONG KONG
SOGO HONG KONG CO., LTD.
銅鑼灣站
Dior
Dior

Levi's
LEVI'S®

Levi's
ORIGINALS LEVI'S ACCESSORIES

Levi's

Levi's

I ♥ levi's

terialand.com
Levi's

Levi's® X Alice Chan / asterialand.com

114″

asteria
© ASTERIA designed by Alice Chan
www.asterialand.com
asterialand
www.asterialand.com

COOL
CREAMY
MIMI
collect them all?
asteria
© ASTERIA designed by Alice Chan www.asterialand.com

115"

116"

**Available in Anna Sui stores

©Alice Chan
TM & © Toy2r(Holdings) Co.Ltd.

adidas

Amy Tollafield

Amy Tollafield, a 21 year-old student originally from North Devon, England, is already an "agitator" within the art world.

This Quentin Tarantino and Tim Burton fan has won various awards, such as Penguin Design Awards 08 and D&AD Awards 08. She likes to create while listening to music, anything depending on her mood and the type of work she is creating at the time.

She enjoys working with collage, paint, ink, fabric and photoshop and ultimately her message is simply "...to let people feel and enjoy positive vibes from my colourful energetic works."
She has been involved with "Let's Stick Together 08," an anti-bullying campaign, for which she created four collectable plushies, each "little creature" with subtle similarities but unique characters too. Her work is an expression and extension of herself, her personality, her fears, things she loves and hates.

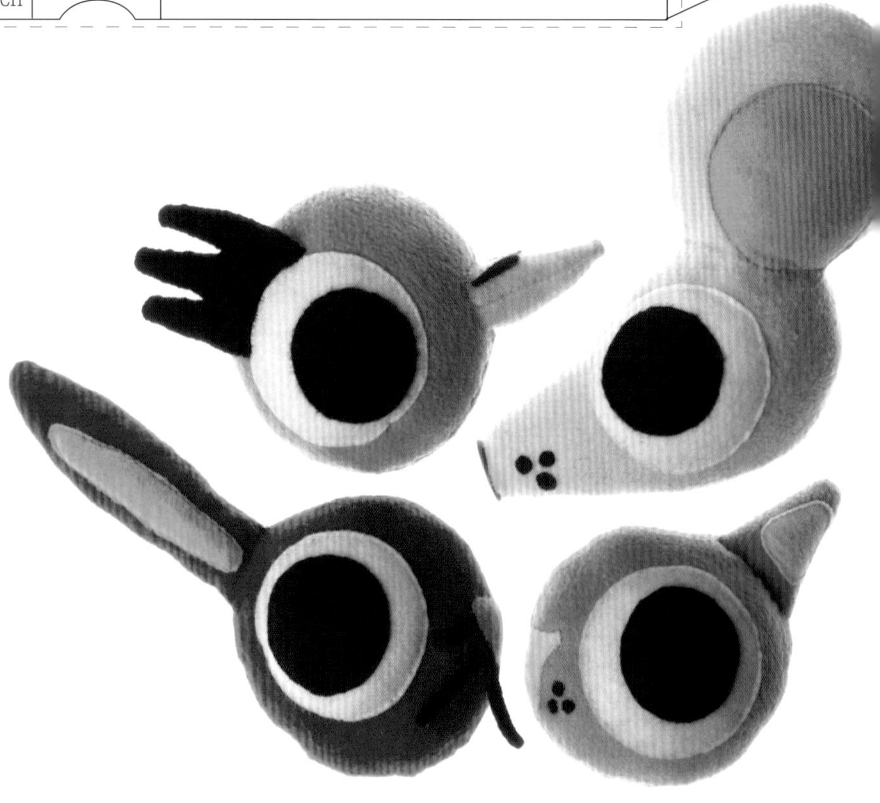

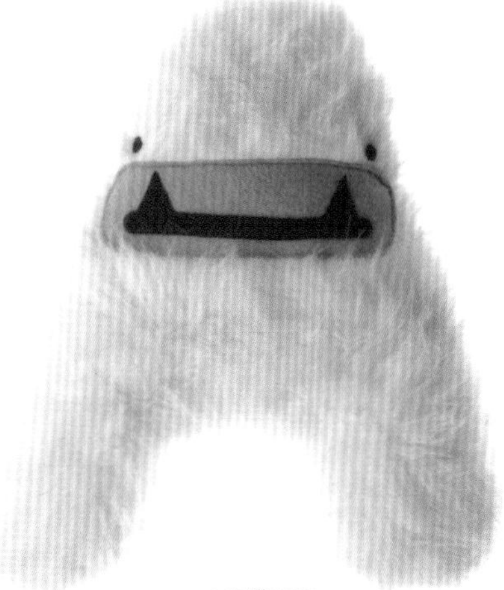

Chad Woodward

A videogame fan, Chad Woodward, is an up-and-coming artist from Devon, England.

A student in Bath, Southern England, Chad is already working for big name companies. He mostly enjoys creating with pen, needle and thread, various toy materials or computer programs such as Photoshop and Illustrator.

He usually generates his ideas through doodling and watching video games, and admits that the secret to realizing his art is "…to just get stuck in". Chad's aim with his work, he tells us, is simply to create "… unique, cute and creepy toys."

121"

Darma Adhitia

Darma Adhitia, aka Darbotz, is one of the most famous designers from Indonesia.
His urban style is his visual identity, and it is prolific across all media sprawling from illustration, apparel, toy design and street art.
As he says, he thinks differently, "... I don't really have methods (for generating ideas), it just flows out of my mind." As unorthodox as his methods, he works well in any media, making an impact and loving everything: spray paint, acrylic, marker, wood, etc.
Darbotz's aim in art is to create icons, trademarks, characters, semiotics, toys... everything acts as a canvas for this Jakartian.

"Explore explore and explore!"

NIKE
26
BE@RBRICK
26°

26°
NIKE
BE@RBRICK

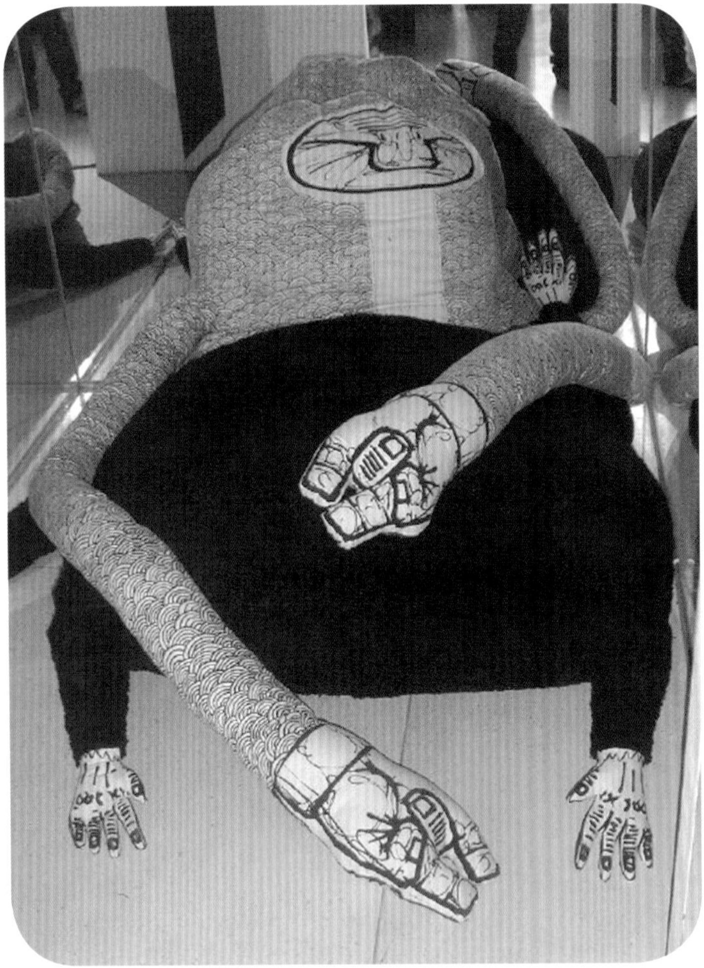

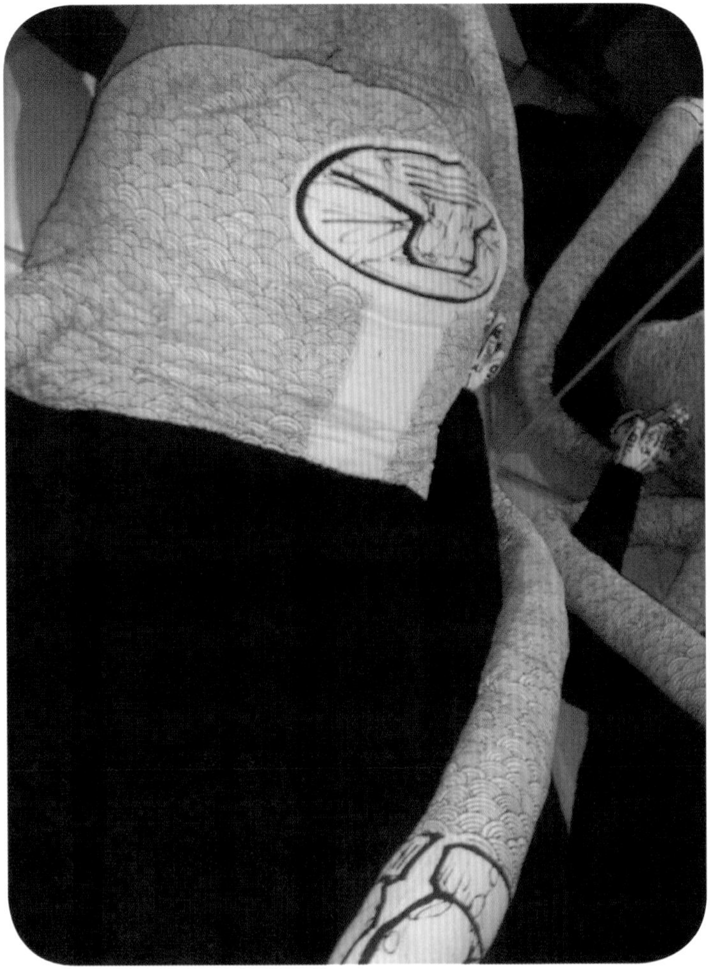

What's The Skinny

Clients and projects you last worked on?

The last one would be a custom bear brick for Nike.

Is there a message in your work or an issue that you want or try to address?

No, it's just my ego.

What do you enjoy about your work?

I enjoy my work because I do what I like, and I am grateful. I love to see people's reactions, and I love it when people love my work or even appreciate it.

Where do you find your inspiration?

My eyes, everything that I see gives me inspiration.

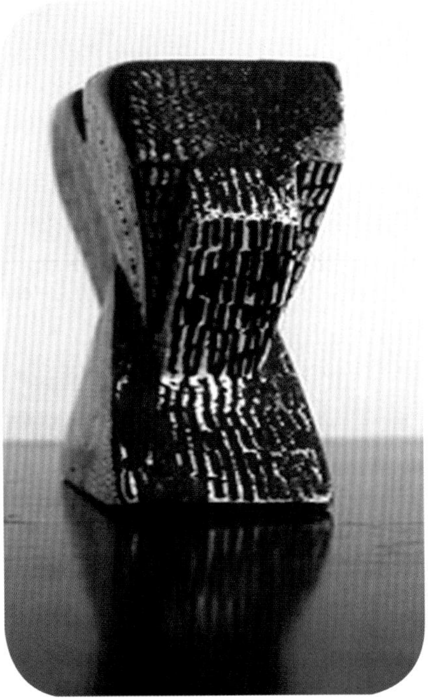

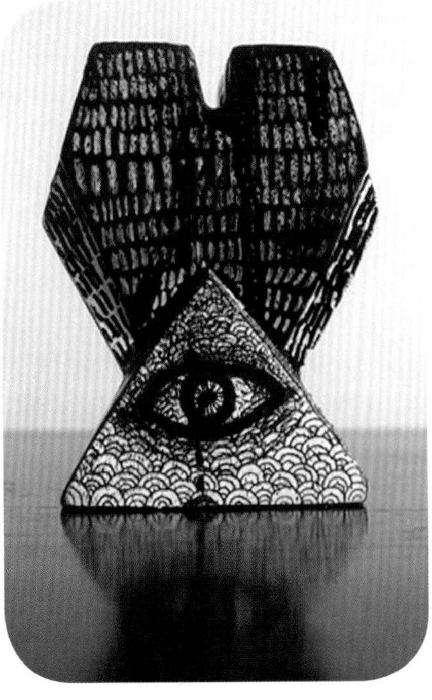

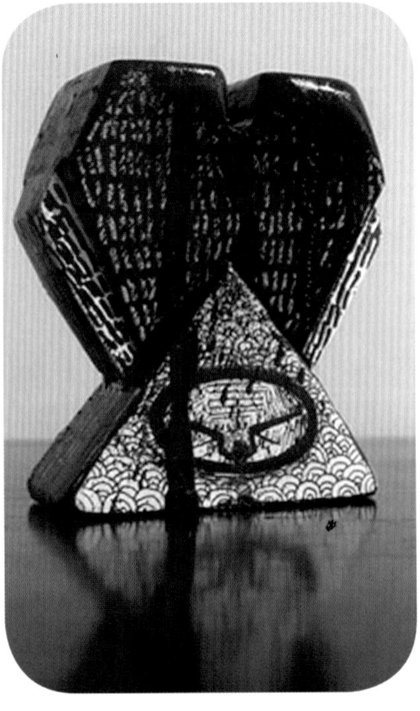

Furi Furi

Furi Furi, a design team based in Tokyo likes to appeal to various audiences across the scope of merchandising, advertising, toy design and other media.

When asked about a preferred media, Tei, a creative director with the company, told us that “As long as I can draw, the type of media is not important.”

Their unique combination of Manga aesthetics with a generous helping of adult madness, best describe this company for whom ‘Team Work’ stands as a daily word... “If I achieved something selfishly it wouldn’t be fun... we generate most of our ideas through communication with others, in meetings with clients, chatting with our staff, conversing with our families,”

This “shaking, swinging” (Furi Furi) company, established in 1998 stands the test of time and breaks through all language barriers globally.

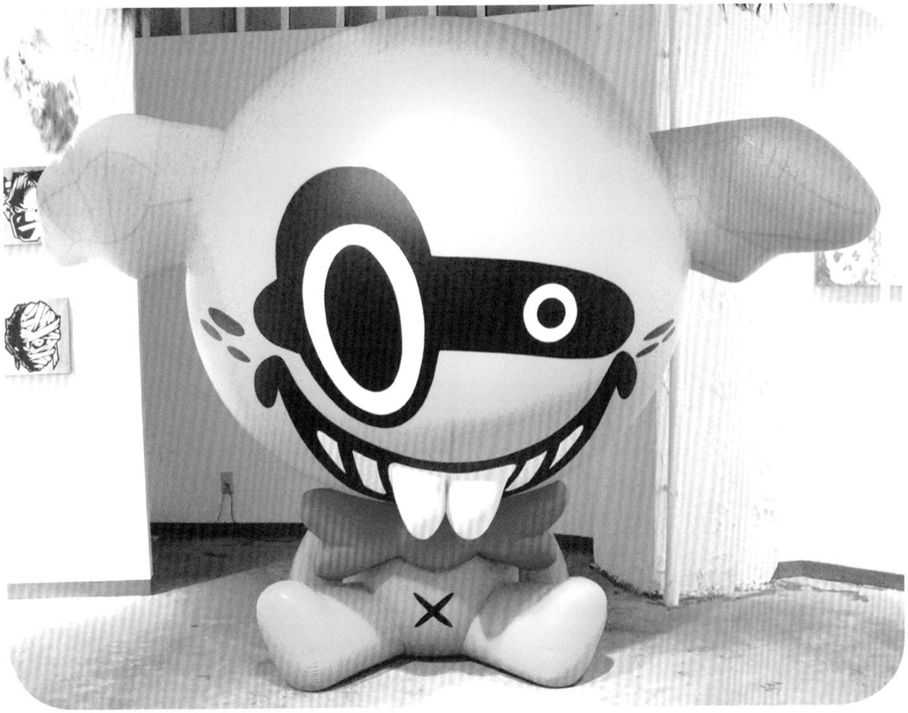

133"

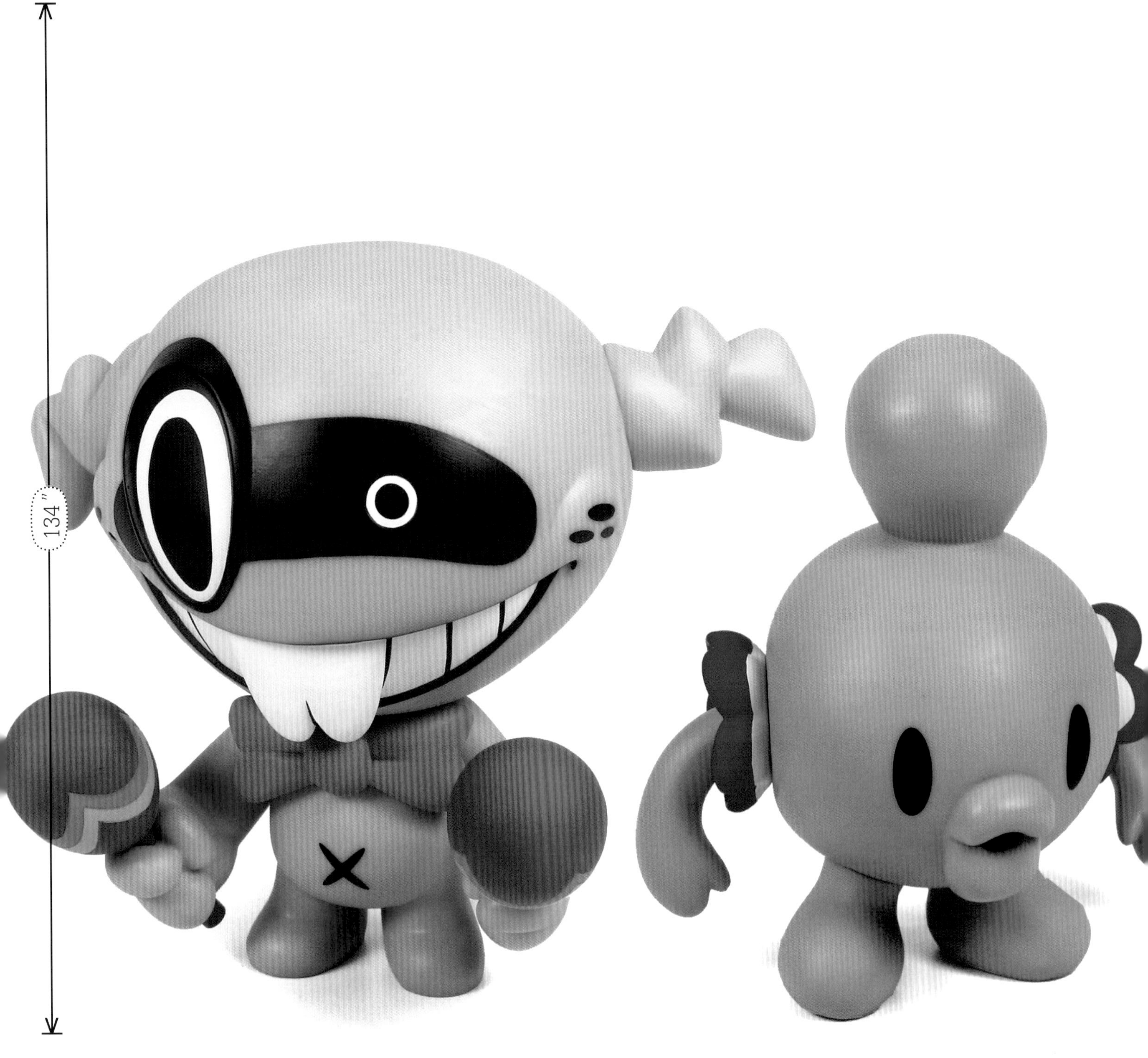
134 "

What's The Skinny

Clients and projects you last worked on?

In Japan, we do total managements of pens from TAKRATOMY called 'PENZGEAR,' and cheesecake shop called 'PODHALE' (of course all the designs too). And in other countries, PV for French DJ, Missille, MID projects for MTV Asia….. I'm really grateful that we have many projects to keep us busy.

Is there a message in your work or an issue that you want or try to address?

To make people happy. This has always been our aim from the start. The results are more important than our own works.

What do you enjoy about your work?

When the people that buy Furi Furi products are satisfied. To make great work, and for no one to pay for it would be a shame... and I would not drink nice SAKE!

Where do you find your inspiration?

From my family, through daily life and the souls of great historical artists.

136”
FATBEAR™

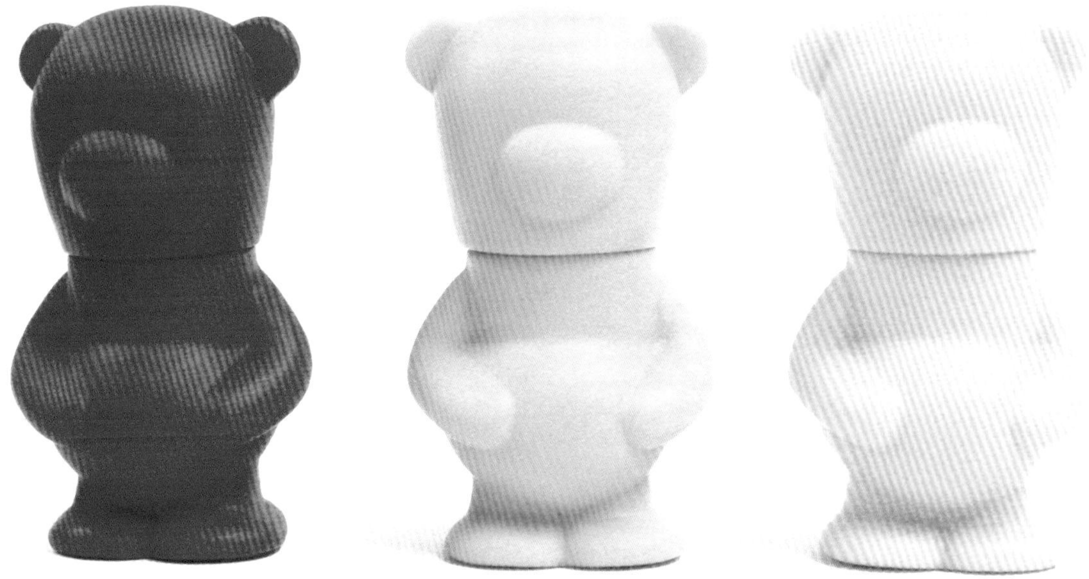

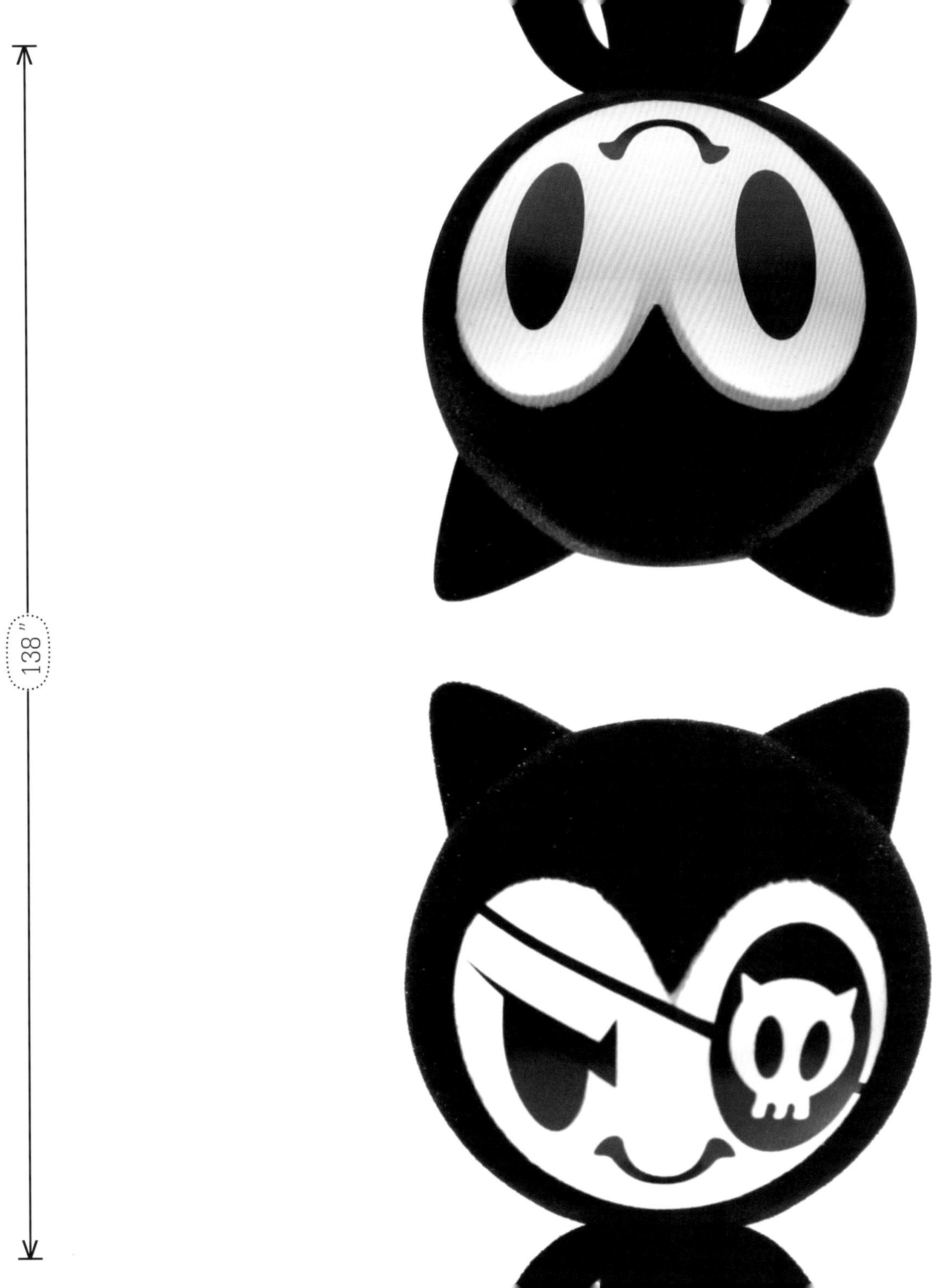
138″

HERE VIL R.I.P.
DO NOT UNSEAL
©FURI FURI COMPANY

DEVIL'S
SWEET
SMILE

142"

FURI
FURI

Gary Baseman

Gary Baseman is a risk taker by nature. This artist from Los Angeles, California, tells us this is one of the best ways for him to generate ideas for his work.

Carrying his sketchbook everywhere, he will arrive at his final creation by "... seeing what themes repeat over and over again in my drawings and this way discover what is on my mind."

Preferring painting to other medias, Gary Baseman feels he has been in the arts all his life. Perhaps for this reason he has made it his work's aim "to discover the secrets about the human condition through art." And he must be the wiser for it...

What's The Skinny

Clients and projects you last worked on?

I created an animated TV show for Disney, I have done handbags, skateboards and theater posters.

Is there a message in your work or an issue that you want or try to address?

My work is all about human desire, longing and lack of control.

What do you enjoy about your work?

I love to discover new truths and watch my art grow through new ideas.

Where do you find your inspiration?

I find inspiration through the air I breathe.

BASEMAN'S
DUNCES

GraphicAirlines

Tat and Vi, better known as GraphicAirlines, came together to form this creative team in 2002. Standing for artistic freedom and creativity, they both consider their aim in art to be "…enjoying the voyage of life's creation. Flying to different realms of creativity is what we hope for. We love to draw in the streets, on trees, on walls, on paper, on wood, on canvas, on clay or in the computer... Everything can act as our canvas."

Doodling and continuous drawing are some of the methods of getting to their creations. As they believe, if you draw everything, even things that don't make sense, then you will get to your final product in a much more spontaneous way.

Tat, who loves to use his pencil and computer, tries not to be "…a money slave and working cow," standing instead for artistic freedom. Viv, a clay figure and acrylic lover, creates art with an insight: "…the fat face with big chests is her icon character. Those fat and big chested characters represent the metropolitan's excessive love for material lives."

These two artists from Hong Kong love to share their art, and so their invitation to everyone continues to be; "Welcome aboard!"

Don't think, just draw.

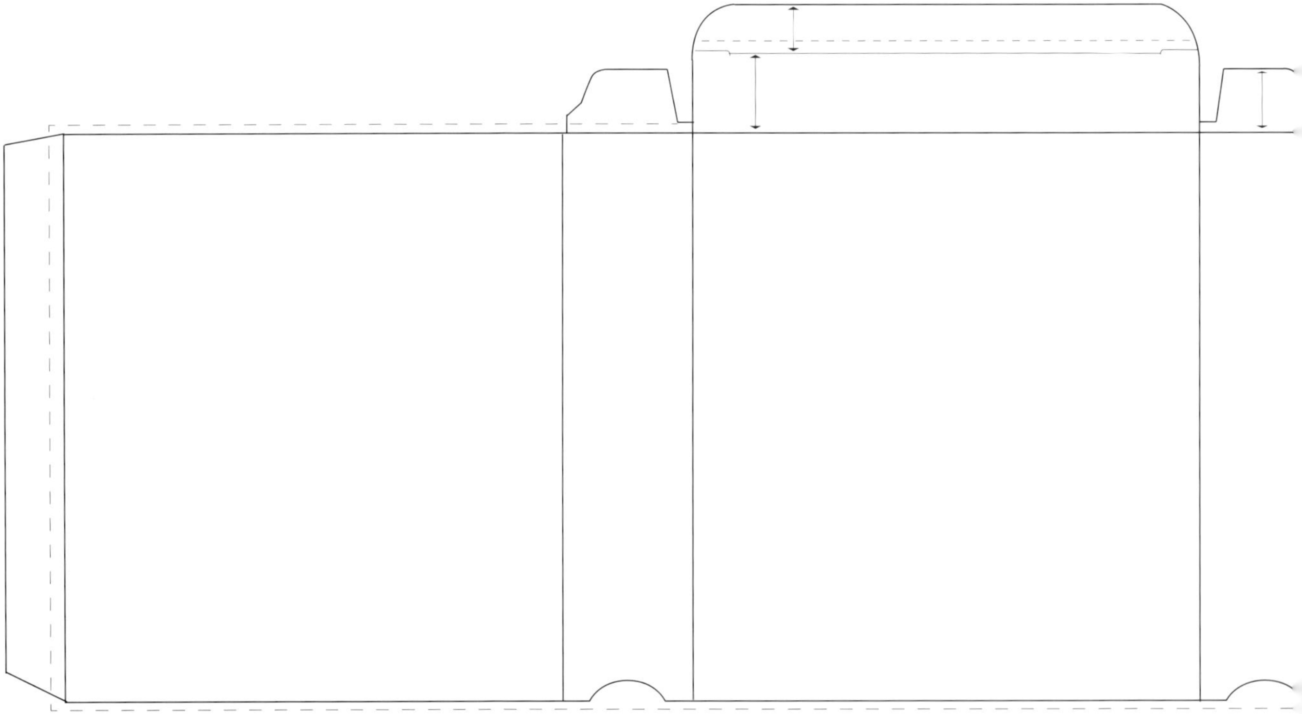

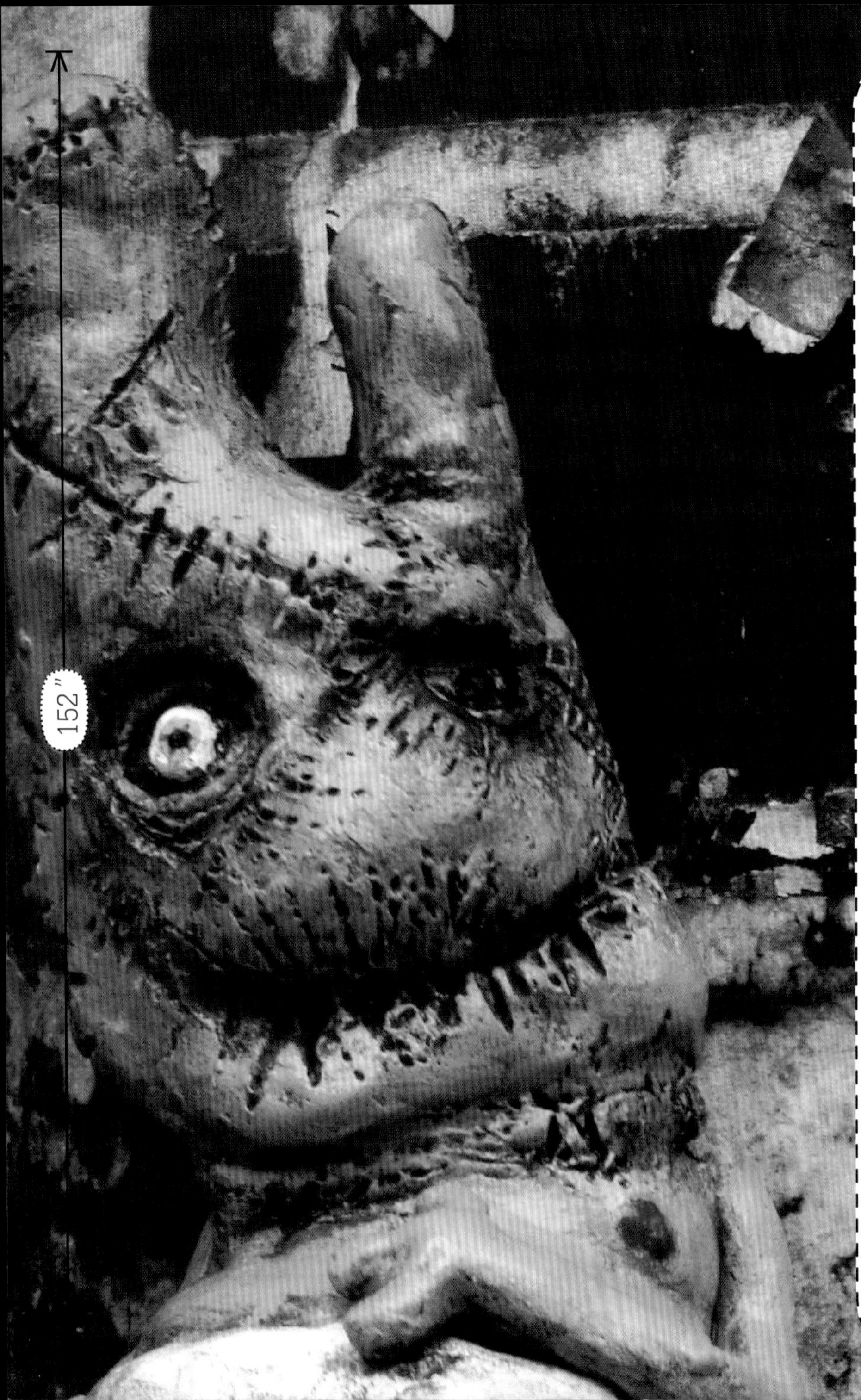

What's The Skinny

Clients and projects you last worked on?

Our latest project is in progress and is our 1st and biggest solo exhibition to date.

Is there a message in your work or an issue that you want or try to address?

Yes, we try to express many different messages in our works.

What do you enjoy about your work?

We enjoy every part of creating. From the first spark of an idea, to following it through to the real thing, and finally seeing people's reactions.

Where do you find your inspiration?

We find inspiration from life, social issues, urban issues, and personal feelings.

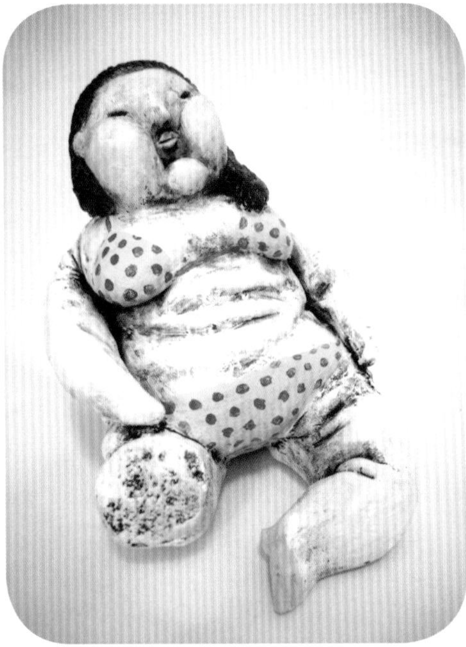

156"

158"
DON't
think

I ♥
HK

Jake

Not a Londoner by birth, Jake originally from Hull, Northern England is a big name in the art scene, working professionally for about 13 years.

The works shown here consist of his 'Badjuju' figures and 'Enough Apes Already,' both of them created with very different aims; 'Badjuju' to make handmade editions that would be as close as possible to factory quality and 'Enough Apes Already' just to "take the piss a bit," as he puts it!

Preferring to use just his pencil, Jake creates most of his works in his sketchbook.

When it comes to designing a new character, he prefers not to use the commonly utilized method of turnaround/technical drawings. Rather, he will make a loose sketch to capture the character's personality, sometimes making a tiny plasticine maquette, or mostly just getting his sculptor Richard Martin, to create a finished sculpture from his drawings.

SURVIVAL OF THE FATTEST
PRINCE FATTY

What's The Skinny

Clients and projects you last worked on?

NME, Esquire, Time Out, Complex, Scratch, Hip-Hop Connection, Graphotism, The Illustrated Ape. I created, wrote and directed a series of animated shorts called 'Geek Boy' for Sci-Fi Channel, and have produced animation for The Mighty Boosh, the BBC, Channel Four and The Samaritans, here in the UK. Last year my work was used extensively for the Star Wars 30th Anniversary events. I continue to work on the Star Wars and Indiana Jones properties for Lucasfilm Ltd. and have designed music packaging for Prodigy, Steinski/Sugarhill Records, Ugly Duckling, Prince Fatty, Fatboy Slim, and others for XL Recordings, Handcuts Records, Mr. Bongo, Antidote, Locked On Recordings etc. I design T-shirts for 2KbyGingham (LA/Tokyo), Gimme 5 Ltd. (London), Five Leaves Inc, Beams T (Tokyo). I collaborated on commercial projects with Colette meets Comme des Garcons, (Paris, Tokyo), Levis, MTV, Motorola, Puma, and Carhartt. I am currently signed to Playbeast (home of Monsterism) for my new range of BADjUjU vinyl figures.

What do you enjoy about your work?

I enjoy the process. I enjoy the excitement of the first spark of an idea. I then struggle with the execution, trying to get what's in my head onto paper. With toys, and directing animation, I can enjoy the finished product and I admire the talent of the sculptors or animators.

Where do you find your inspiration?

At inconvenient times and in the unlikeliest places. But music and Japan seem to be two recurring sources of inspiration.

enough
apes
already
enough
apes
already
another JAKe ape®
colettemeets
COMME des GARÇONS
*
adFunture x colettemeetsCOMMEdesGARÇONS x JAKe

enough
apes
already
enough
apes
already

enough
apes
already
163 "

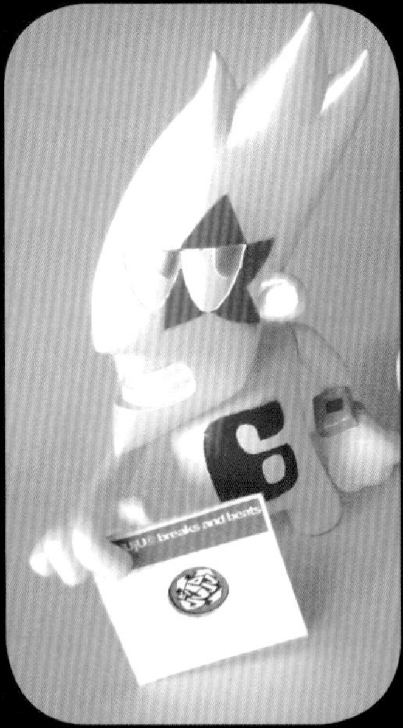
breaks and beats

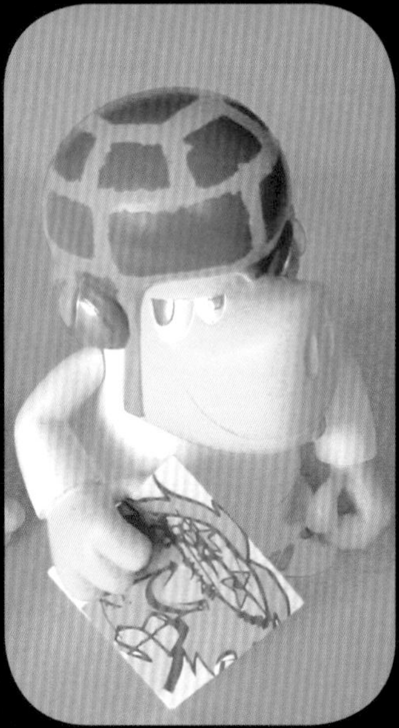

in STEREO
MILK AND HONEY
PRINCE FATTY

S IS FOR
STANLEY

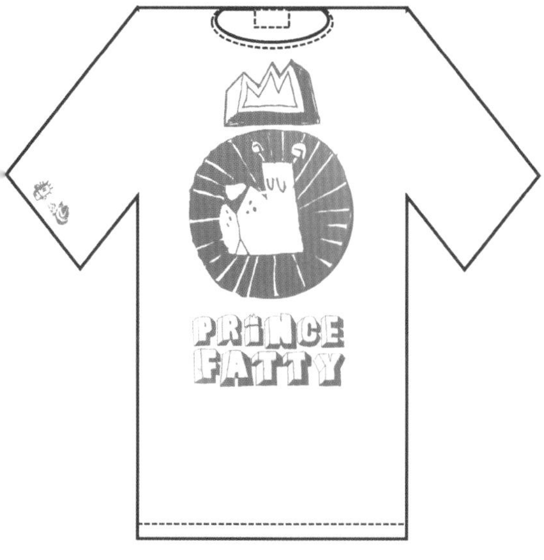
PRINCE
FATTY

STAR
WARS
STAR WARS
CELEBRATION IV
© 2007 Lucasfilm Ltd. & TM
www.jake-art.com

Sillyivy

Liu Yang, from Shanghai, approaches her work in a very human way, "they are not perfect, each of my works has a little flaw, just like our lives and our hearts.

Sillyivy.com, her website, shows us just this, along with her characteristic practicality.

Every time she creates, she always tries to make her work into something real, usable and touchable. But with along all this, her aim is still for the "passenger" who sees her art, buys her art, likes her art... to take away an emotion, the emotion that her work awakens.

I LOVE

I LOVE LV
People Like Me
Studio

SketOne

Andrew Yasgar, aka SketOne, considers calm as his main work method. Not surprising for someone who comes from "Money Kravin, Pistol Wavin, New Haven, Connecticut USA," as he puts it!

He has been involved in the arts since childhood and usually likes to use paper and pencil as his preferred media to create. With those, he works on his ideas and then always goes back and reviews everything.

But mainly his focus stays on showing versatility; "Thinking beyond a box, circle or whatever shape you try to contain me in."

"World domination!"

170 ''

HEINZ
1886
BEANS
with tomato sauce
13.7 OZ(385g)

HEINZ
57
VARIETIES
HEINZ
1869
TOMATO
KETCHUP
NET WT 14 OZ-397 g

HP
SAUCE
HP
SAUCE
THE Original

What's The Skinny

Clients and projects you last worked on?

Kidrobot, Wheaty Wheat, Red Magic and Kaching Brands.

Is there a message in your work or an issue that you want or try to address?

Fun!

What do you enjoy about your work?

I like the method of creating my works and the reactions of those that come in touch with it.

Where do you find your inspiration?

Everywhere!

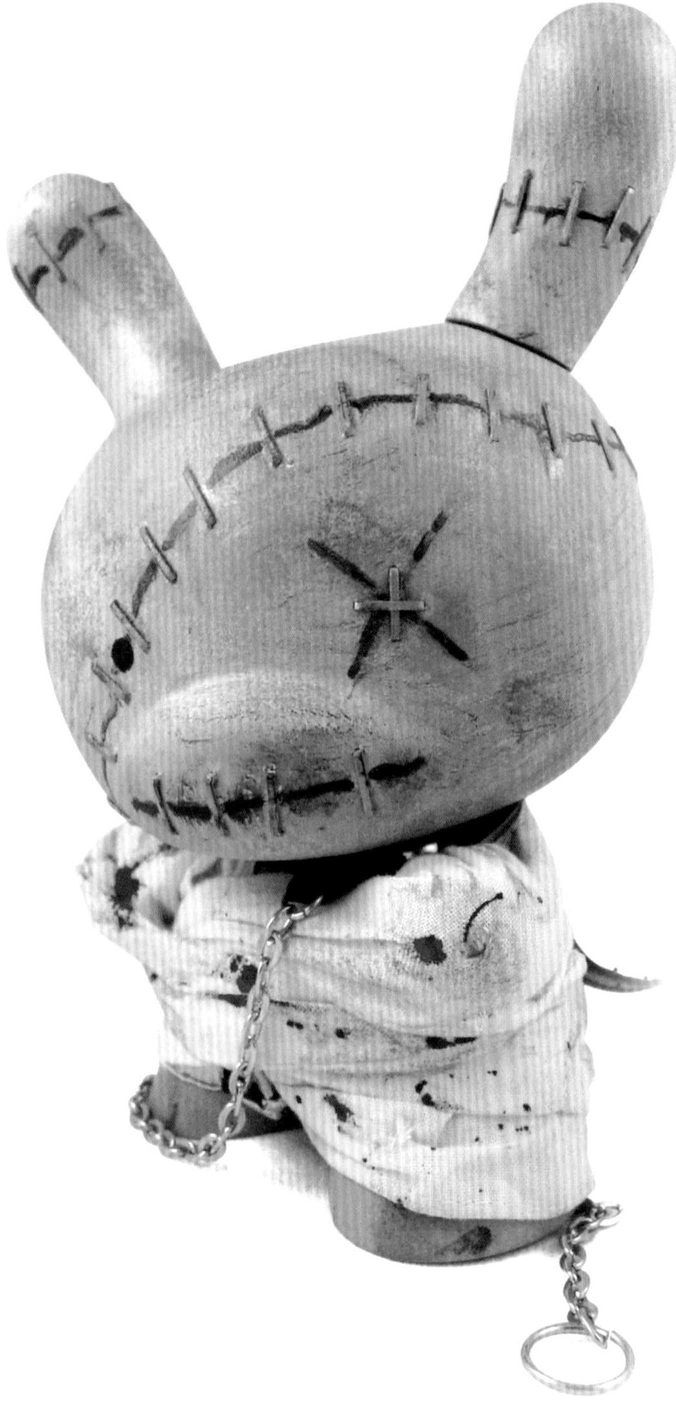

LOOSE BOLTS
SPARE RIBS
BROKEN HEART
BUCKET FOOT

POLICE DEPARTMENT
NYPD
POLICE

178"

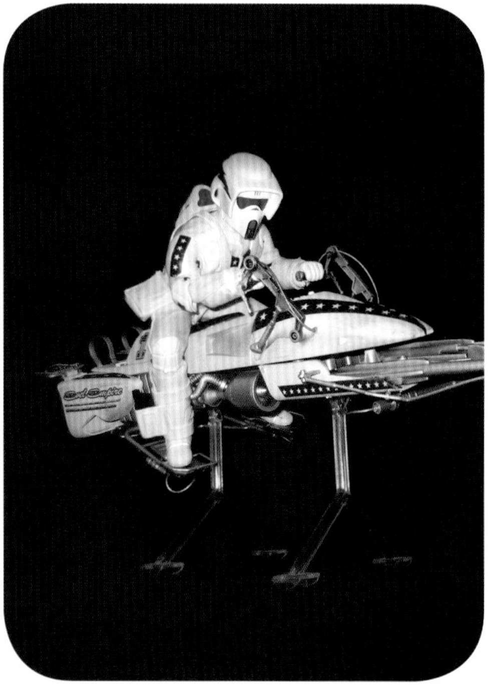

BRANDED
Superior

Ripple
FLAVORWAY
CHOKING HAZARD
sket one
181"

Tokidoki

Simone Legno is the artistic vision behind Tokidoki. Having started out just as an online portfolio for this Italian artist, Tokidoki now ranges from a variety of apparel, art and lifestyle products. These include: a clothing line, vinyl toys, art-skateboards, pin badges, iSkins, jewelry, watches, knitwear, sportswear, accessories, shoes, stationery and much more. Having moved to LA from his hometown of Rome in 2004, Simone Legno together with his business partners, have managed to establish a major illustration, advertising and new media design brand.

A lover of Japan and all its diversity, Simone Legno uses his work as a life diary, drawing inspiration and generating ideas just by watching the world around him and filtering all the valuable information That is already there.

www.strangeco.com

tokidoki
ADIOS
ciao ciao
183"

184"

186"
I
LA

tokido
I LA
LA
187"

tokidoki for Hello Kitty

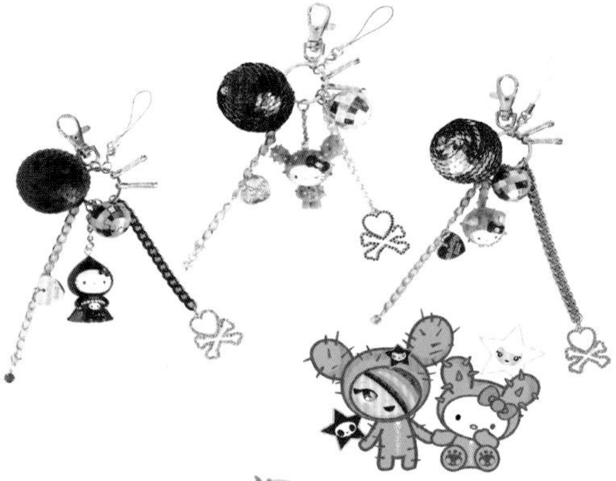

ADIOS
latte
tokidoki

....loves me!

192"

What's The Skinny

Clients and projects you last worked on?

The second season of tokidoki for Onitsuka tiger, more tokidoki X Hello Kitty, tokidoki soccerball with MIKA-SA, tokidoki made in italy shoes, new toys, new clothing and bags etc. Always a lot going on.

Is there a message in your work or an issue that you want or try to address?

Be positive and believe that what you really dream can really happen if do your best to achieve it.

What do you enjoy about your work?

The fact that I can wear and be fully immersed in my design.

Where do you find your inspiration?

People, traveling, anything around me.

"Cute characters are reinterpretations of reality in an original and personal way. As a logo they need design skills of synthesis and as art pieces they are wonderful conveyors of feelings the artist wants to express."

tokidoki
....loves me!
....loves me not
latte
I LA
www.tokidoki.it

ADIOS
ciao ciao

ciao ciao
ADIOS

ADIOS
ciao
ciao

tokidoki

BE@RBRICK
Gooal!
Gooal!

Onitsuka
Tiger

W

203"

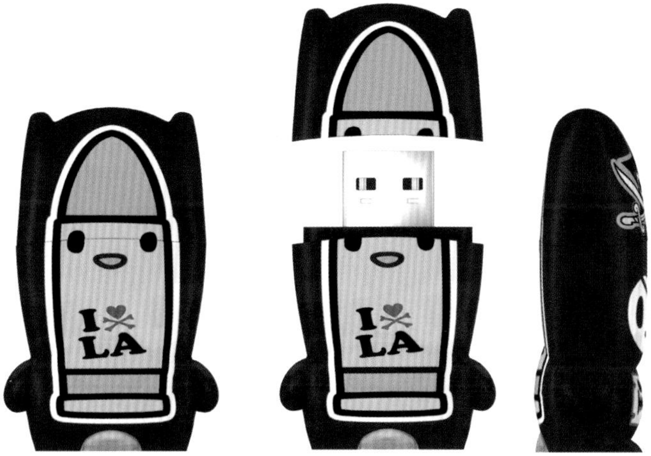
I LA
I LA

Jason Siu

Having stumbled upon character design, Jason Siu is now an eminent figure in the Asian design world, best described by his urban hip hop art style.

He draws on experiences from his daily life to generate ideas and concepts, and to express his own mind is always his main goal. His work expands from toys, to paintings, illustrations and even comic work.

He owns his own company, Jason Siu&Co, and feels that both Western and Asian concepts and icons influence his works. Things like the cities around him and all their related issues, such as repressed racism and cultural communities, greatly affect greatly his art.

"I really believe that any art performance can make the world perfect & enhance the civilization of people."

207

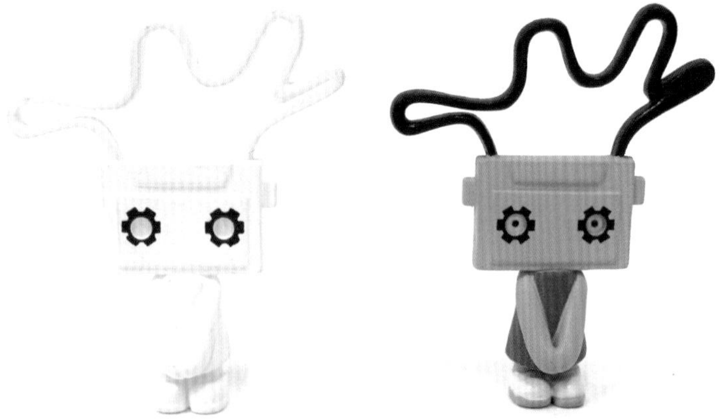

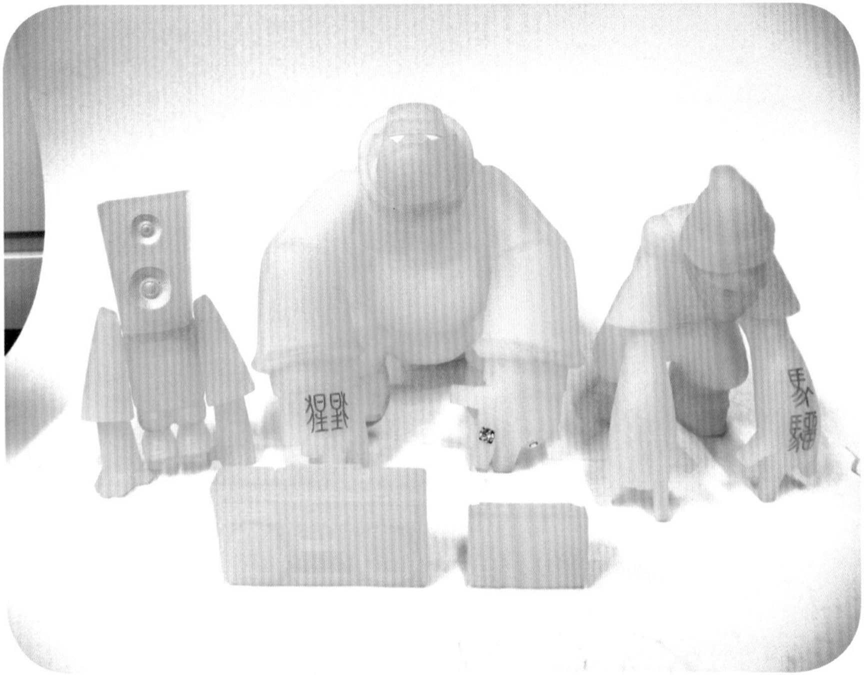

What's The Skinny

Clients and projects you last worked on?

Sony, Pepsi, Burger King….

Is there a message in your work or an issue that you want or try to address?

Yes, an example is "Speak Your Mind."

What do you enjoy about your work?

I enjoy people's response to the concepts behind my works.

Where do you find your inspiration?

From lots of sources, e.g. experiences, daily life, books, films….

50 Cent's
you almost
make a perfect couple. But
RECORD DON'T MAKE NO CA
SECOND-MOST-SUCCESSFU
BOY IN HIP
HIS MENTOR
www.omerta

Rabe di Koppa

fresh

fresh

three zero
threezero

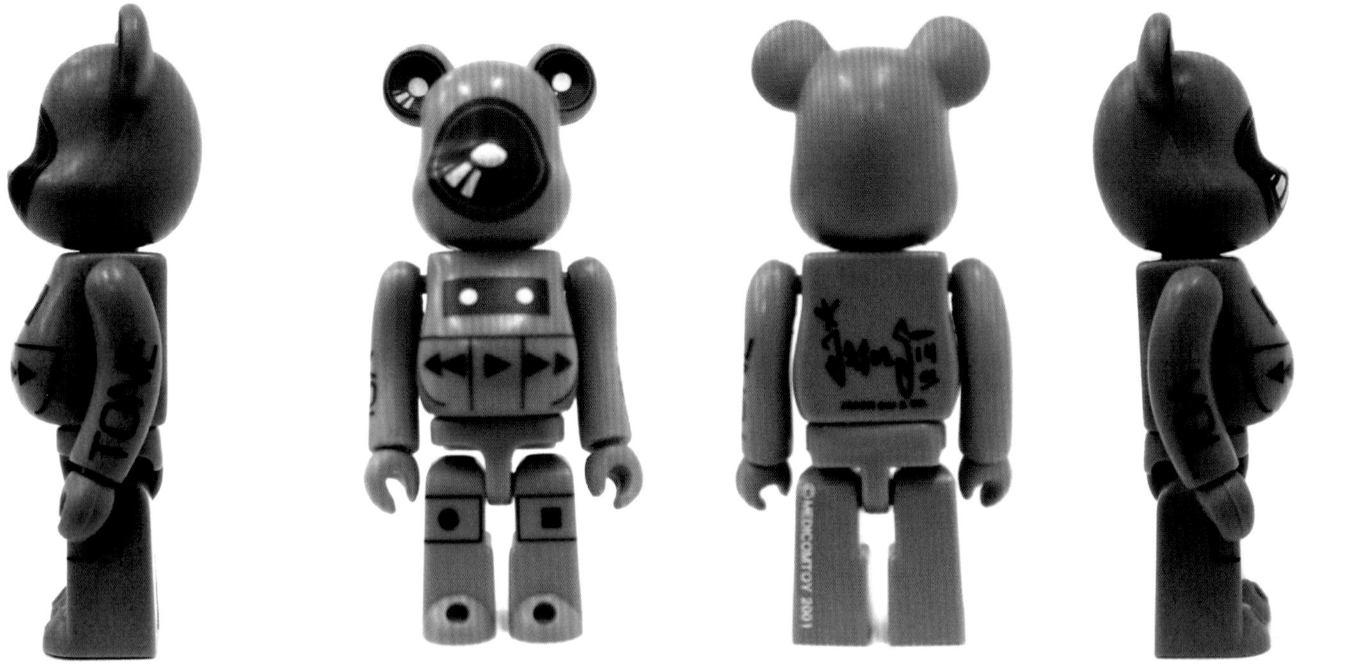

212"

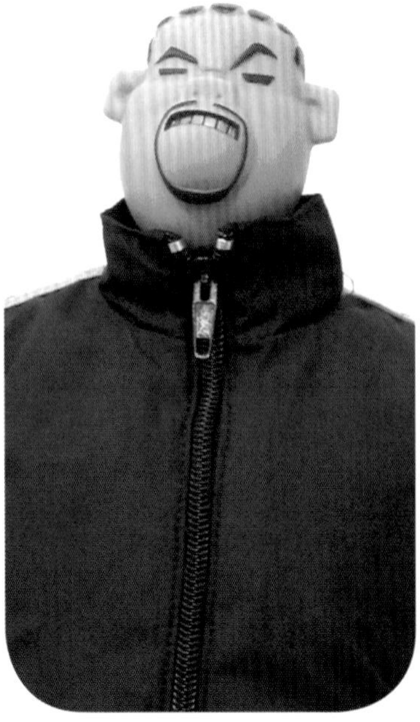

GANGSTER PARADISE
GANGSTER
GANGSTER PARADISE
JOKER

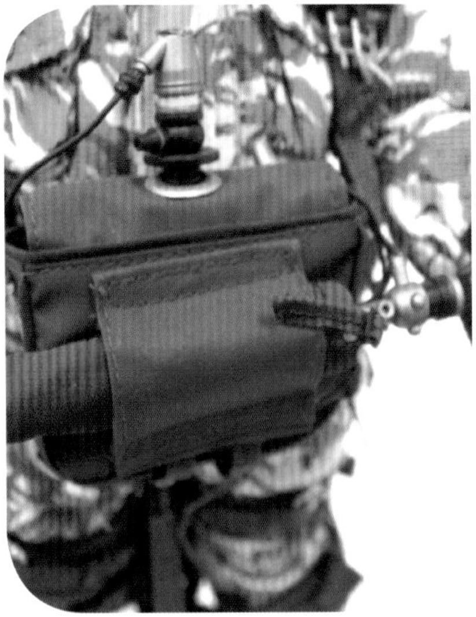

three zen

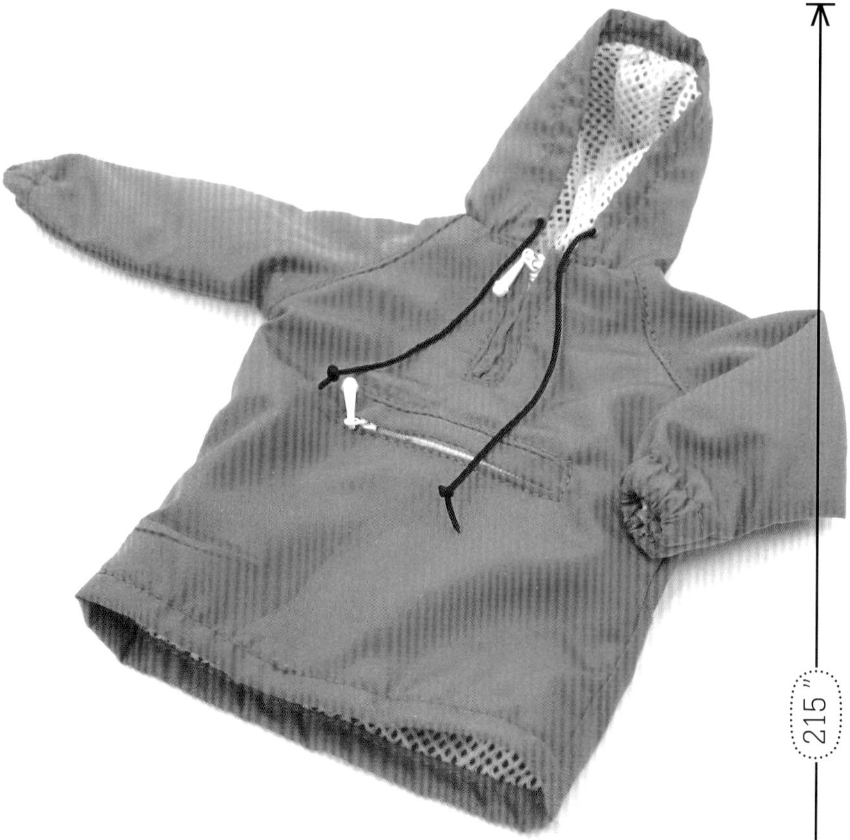

BRONX
N.Y.

NEW YORK

80
FUNKY
#1 DJ DOM
Le sillion de la culture
Hip hop

Le sillon de la culture
hip hop
DJ BATTLE
FUNKY
DJ BATTLE
MUSIC FOR
THE MATURE B-BOY

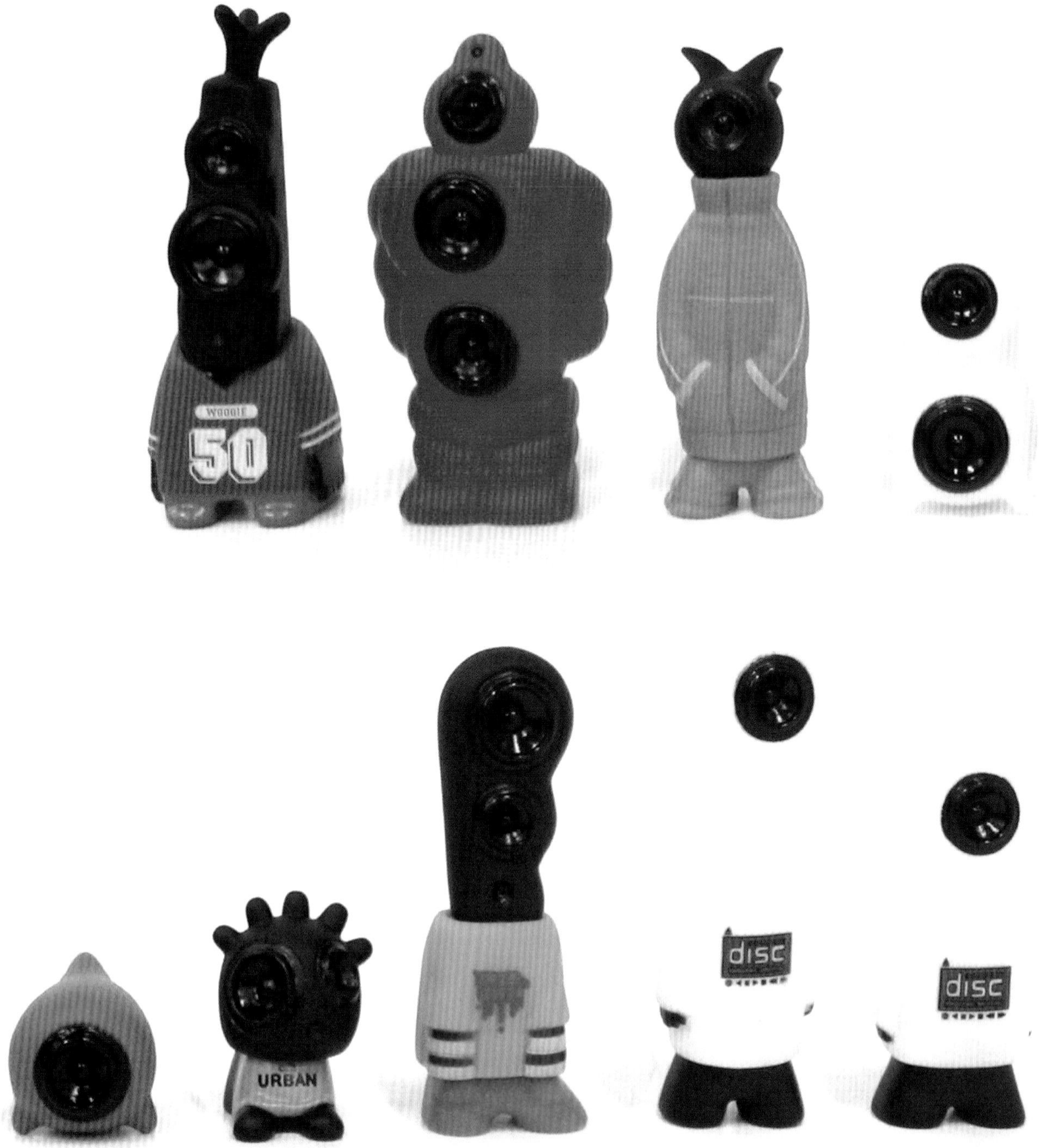
WOOGIE
50
URBAN
disc
disc

disc
URBAN
WOOGIE
50

220"
JOKER
68

THREE

Angels and Gringos

Mainly a sculptor, Daniel Monahan, better known as "Angels and Gringos," his company name, tells us a lot of his work ideas and concepts have been affected by Mexican culture.

Growing up near the border in San Diego, California, he was exposed to a lot of Day of The Dead, or Dia De Los Muertos, celebrations.

Together with his love for the famous story of Don Quixote, these were two of the thoughts behind one of his characters shown in this book: Sancho.

Preferring to work with plastic and bronze, Daniel Monahan has a very specific way of arriving at his final 'work of art,'

"I first start off with a really loose sketch. It helps me to discover the concepts and forms that will make it into the sculpture. From there I build a firm wire frame, or armature, that I can model the clay on top of. Then I work from imagination to realize the final piece, constantly working and reworking the shapes. Then I divide the sculpture into pieces and make a silicone mold from which I can cast master castings to send to the factory. There they use my model along with the Illustrator color files I send them, to put the piece into production."

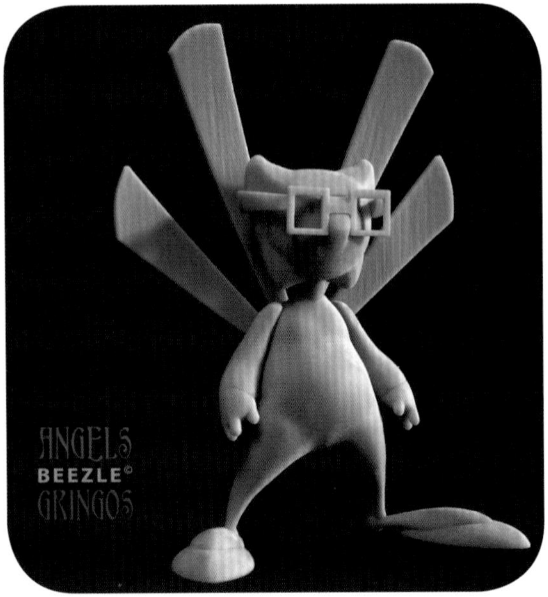

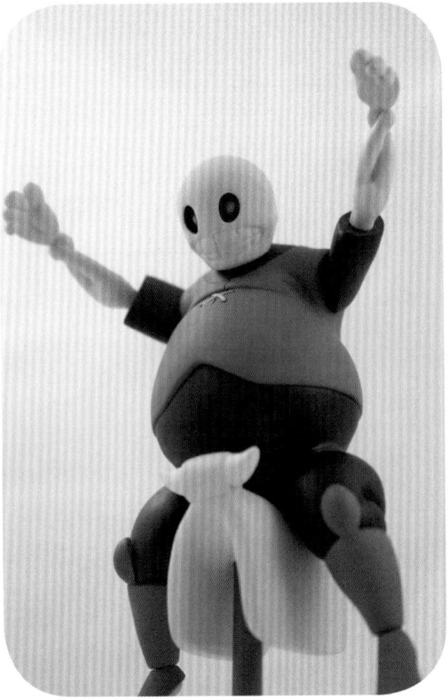

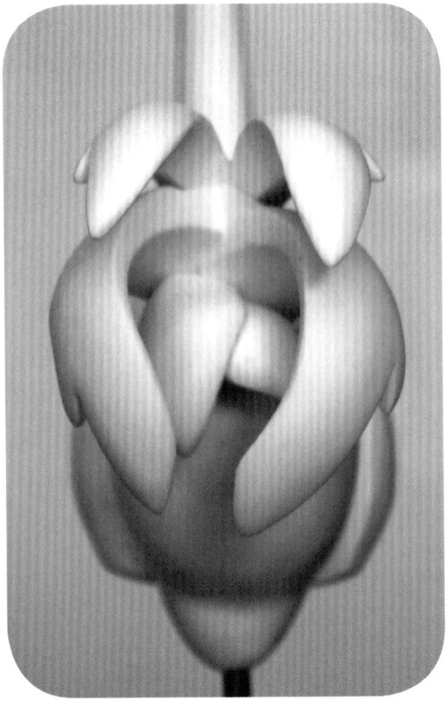

What's The Skinny

Clients and projects you last worked on?

Most of my clients are either in the animation or fine art industries. I do a lot of fabrication work for some of the bigger names in the fine art world. Many of the same processes used to create high-profile installations are the ones used to create my vinyl art.

Is there a message in your work or an issue that you want or try to address?

I like working in vinyl because it makes art into an experience. It can be touched, manipulated, and played with in a way that most traditional artworks can't. It applies to the kinesthetic aspects of expression and creativity that for many people are more impacting than visual ones.

What do you enjoy about your work?

The thing I enjoy most is the creative process, getting to introduce a new character into the world that didn't exist before. The fact that people like my work is a huge bonus, but I think that I'd still do it even if I were on my own.

Where do you find your inspiration?

My inspiration comes from all over. You'll never know when something you see or experience in everyday life will become the catalyst for a work of art.

Kenny Wong

An artist with a mission, Kenny Wong, wants to make a difference with his work.

Having been in the arts for almost 20 years, this 'Hong Kongneser,' uses sketching and clay carving as his main methods to realizing his art, while enjoying the use of 3D design and graphic image. But as he puts it, he prefers "…to use the human being's image to express my idea."

In a way, he identifies himself with his characters, as they come from his everyday life and issues that worry him such as environmental protection, which is a very urgent issue to him.

"When I was little, I had a lot of dreams and imagination about the ocean and its life; this is how Copperhead-18 (one of his characters) comes out. One day I met a very interesting kid on a beneficial painting exhibition, and that inspired me to create Molly."

Molly
HK

Molly
Molly
Molly

Molly
K

230"
M

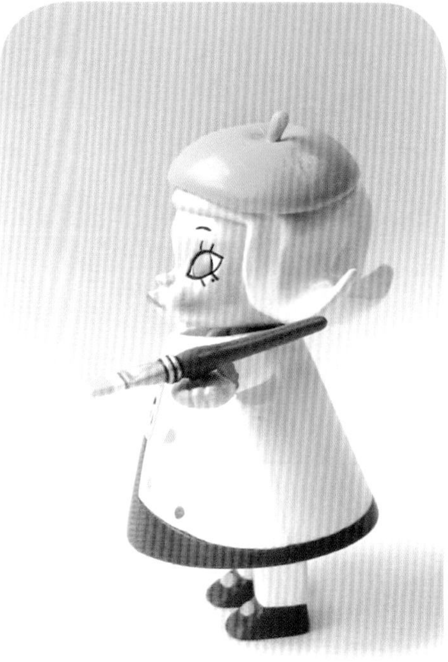

What's The Skinny

Clients and projects you last worked on?

I just finished a Levi's and Medicom series. Now I'm working on a new exhibition for Sun Hung Kai & Co. Limited and Mollympic.

Is there a message in your work or an issue that you want or try to address?

No one can deny our childhood, a beautiful age when we can freely express our happiness, anger, and all kinds of feelings. We've all had beautiful dreams, expressing our pure feelings through a pencil. But all the study and hard work have made us so stressed, and we are lost. We forget ourselves, our friends, our life, even forget how to love. Even little kids have to accommodate this fast modern life, by practicing piano, dancing, tests. Where is their innocence? No one cares. I believe, we all have a child within us, and we are all eager to have love and have the ability to express love. Molly is trying to remind us of that, don't just stay still, add some imagination, flying with our dream from childhood.

Where do you find your inspiration?

Molly is a very funny character in real life. I remember one day I took part in a benefit painting exhibition as an illustrator, and the host asked us and the children to draw each other. I tried my best. I found one little kid paid all his attention to draw me, looking at me carefully with his pretty eyes, as clear as the lake. He is more serious than any professional illustrators there. So this super cute character comes out.

Pee
Pee
K
K
K

Molly

234"
最愛豆腐
kennyswork all rights reserved
www.kennyswork.com
All rights reserved by kennyswork
Molly
Molly the painter
kennyswork all rights reserved
www.kennyswork.com
nice to meet you
kennyswork all rights reserved
www.kennyswork.com

MOLLY
Molly

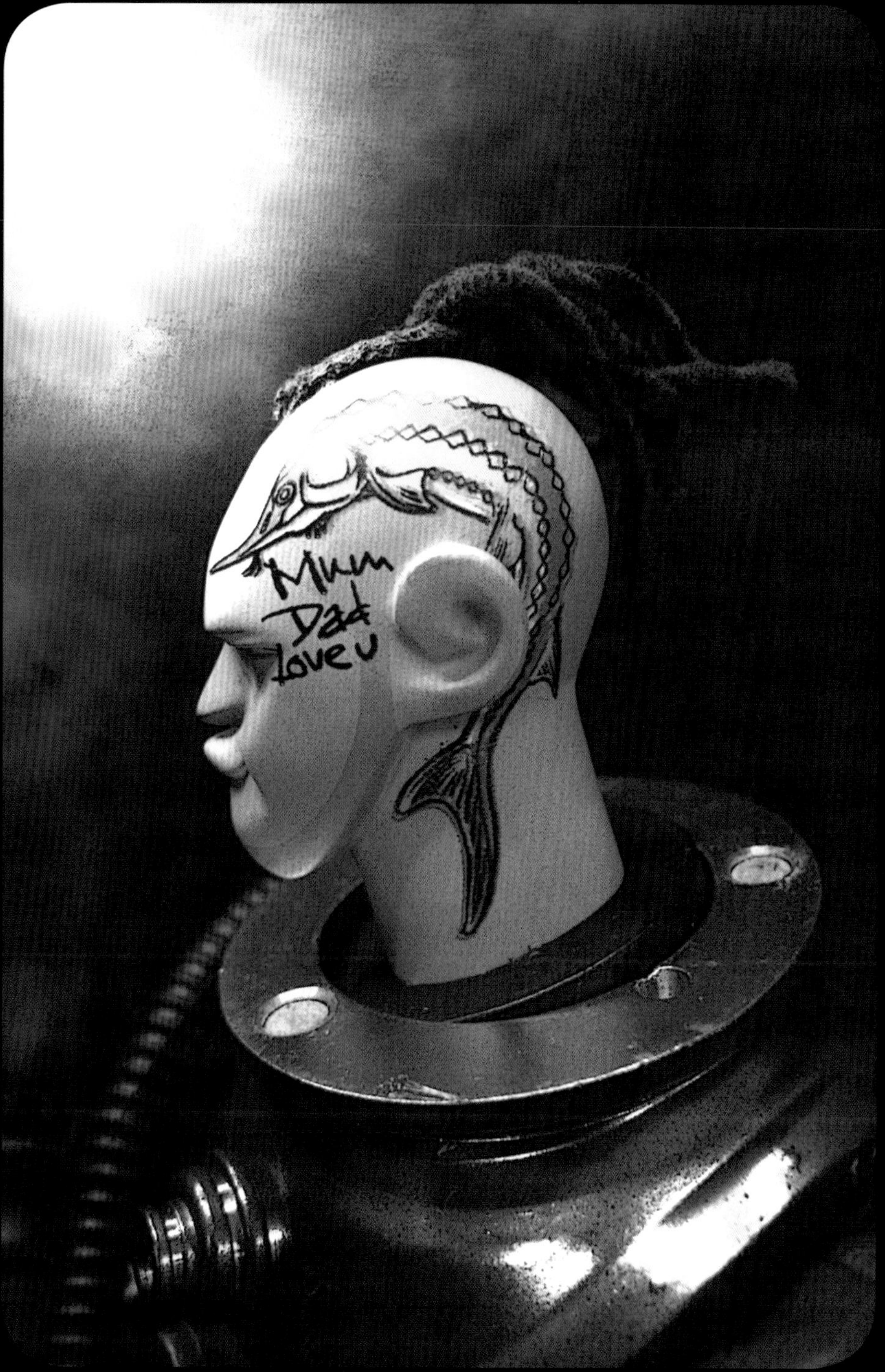
Mum
Dad
love u

238"

239"

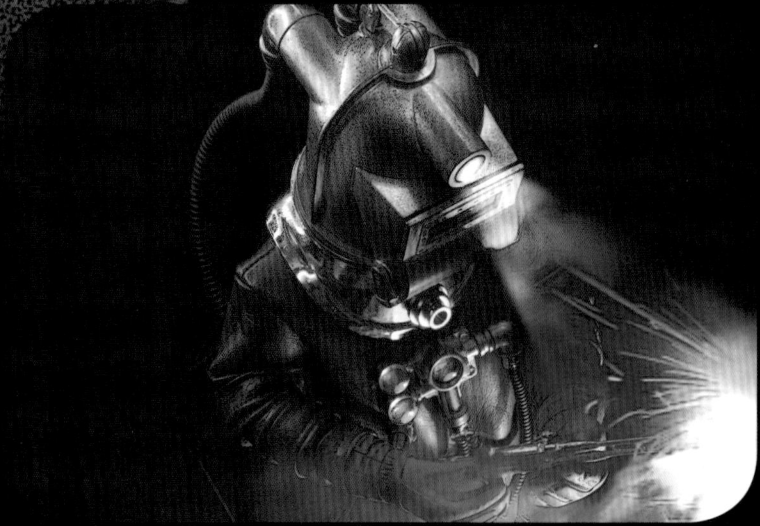

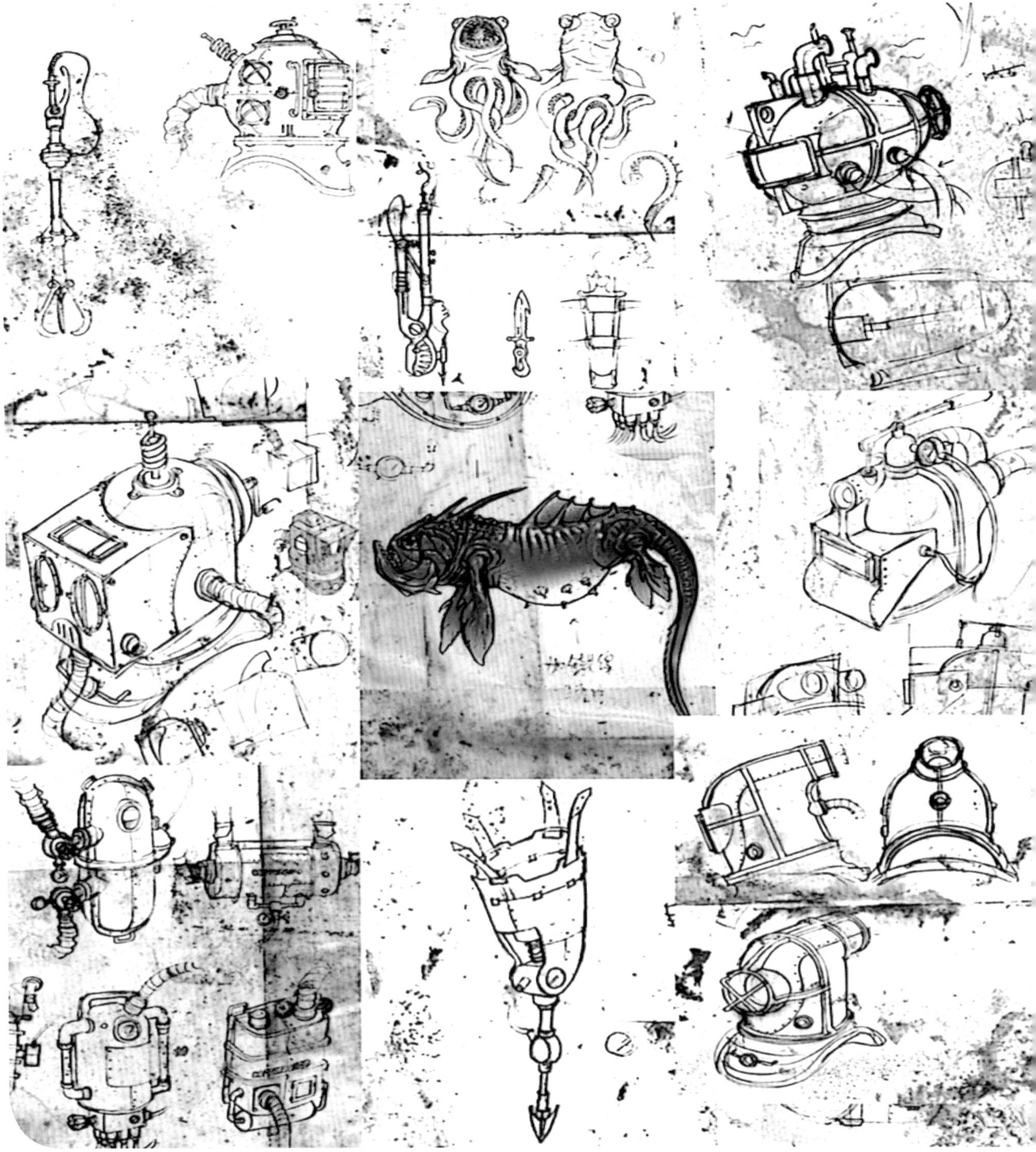

242"

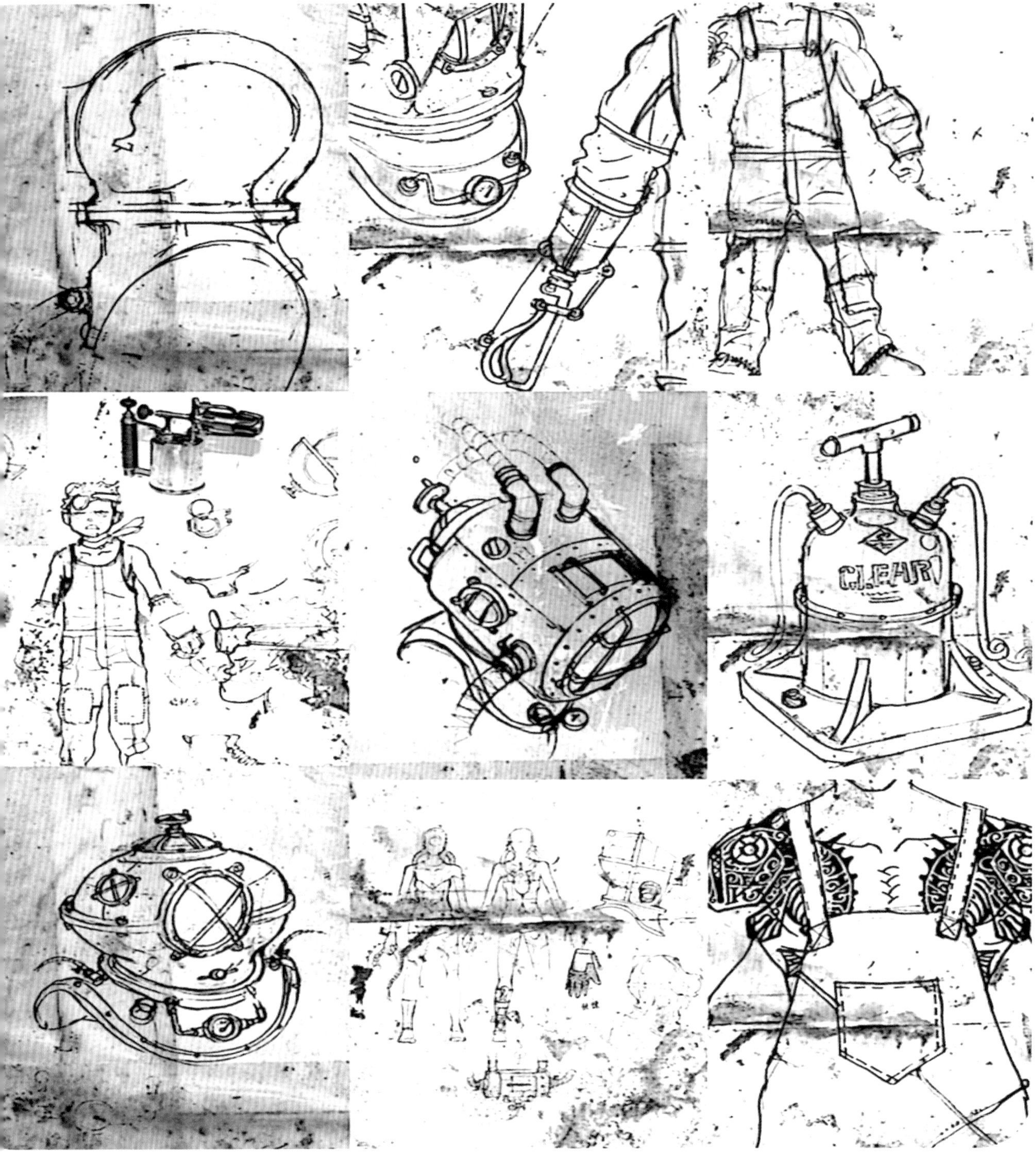
CLEAR

Jeremyville

Dividing his time and work between Sydney, Australia and New York, Jeremyville actually studied architecture at university, before finding his niche.

Nowadays, he stands as one of the most respected artists across media, with his work being found from coast to coast.

As a cross media artist, Jeremyville chooses the media that will be the most relevant for each piece such as: drawing, animation, large painting, apparel, product design, the written word, quick sketches, elaborate drawings, murals, collage, and toy design.

To be unique, different and "true to his own voice" is the most important thing to him.

He also loves to just draw and takes his sketchbook around with him, though generating his best ideas at night time, at candlelight with his pen and sketchbook.

"It's important for me to be true to who I am, and to be original."

SOUL TRAIN
FOREVER
I'M OKAY YOU'RE OKAY
LET LOVE IN
let go.
you're amongst friends
OPEN UP!
STAY FURRY
RISE UP!
JEREMY VILLE
let love in...
GROW YER OWN...
I could be here forever...
LET'S SCRIBBLE!
TWEEDLE!
NEW!
UNITE! DON'T UNTIE!
MORE JAZZ
petting zoo
IT'S ALL GOOD...
ANARCHIST IN FURS
98% WOOL
OPEN 25hours
ROCK ON!
LINT
JEREMY VILLE
jeremyville
KEEP IT REAL

245"

What's The Skinny

Clients and projects you last worked on?

Converse shoes by Jeremyville, Rossignol snowboards by Jeremyville, toys with Kidrobot, STRANGEco, my 2 books Vinyl Will Kill and Jeremyville Sessions, published by IdN. MTV animation, I was invited to paint a toy for MTV Italy in Milan 07. I was also invited to be a part of Tiger Translate in Beijing 2007. i was in a group show at Colette in Paris in 2007.

Is there a message in your work or an issue that you want or try to address?

To try and tap into my subconscious thoughts and dreamlike state. I describe my work as Acid Pop.

What do you enjoy about your work?

Being true to the initial idea in my head.

Where do you find your inspiration?

Under a secret mushroom in a far away forest.

JEREMY
VILLE

JEREMY
VILLE
25 HOURS

FAN
01

FAN
01

FAN
01

248"

geee...
wowww...
greaaaat...
Ghost of ANDY
jeremyville
Ghost of ANDY
jeremyville
black white 225 551 549 507 509

wowww...
Ghost of ANDY

LOSS
DEATH
IN MY HEAD
CARNAGE
DECAY
VENGEANCE

LOST
SCOUTS OF
JEREMYVILLE
...where
am I ?
SCOUTS

...where
am I ?
SCOUTS
LOST
SCOUTS OF
JEREMYVILLE

252"

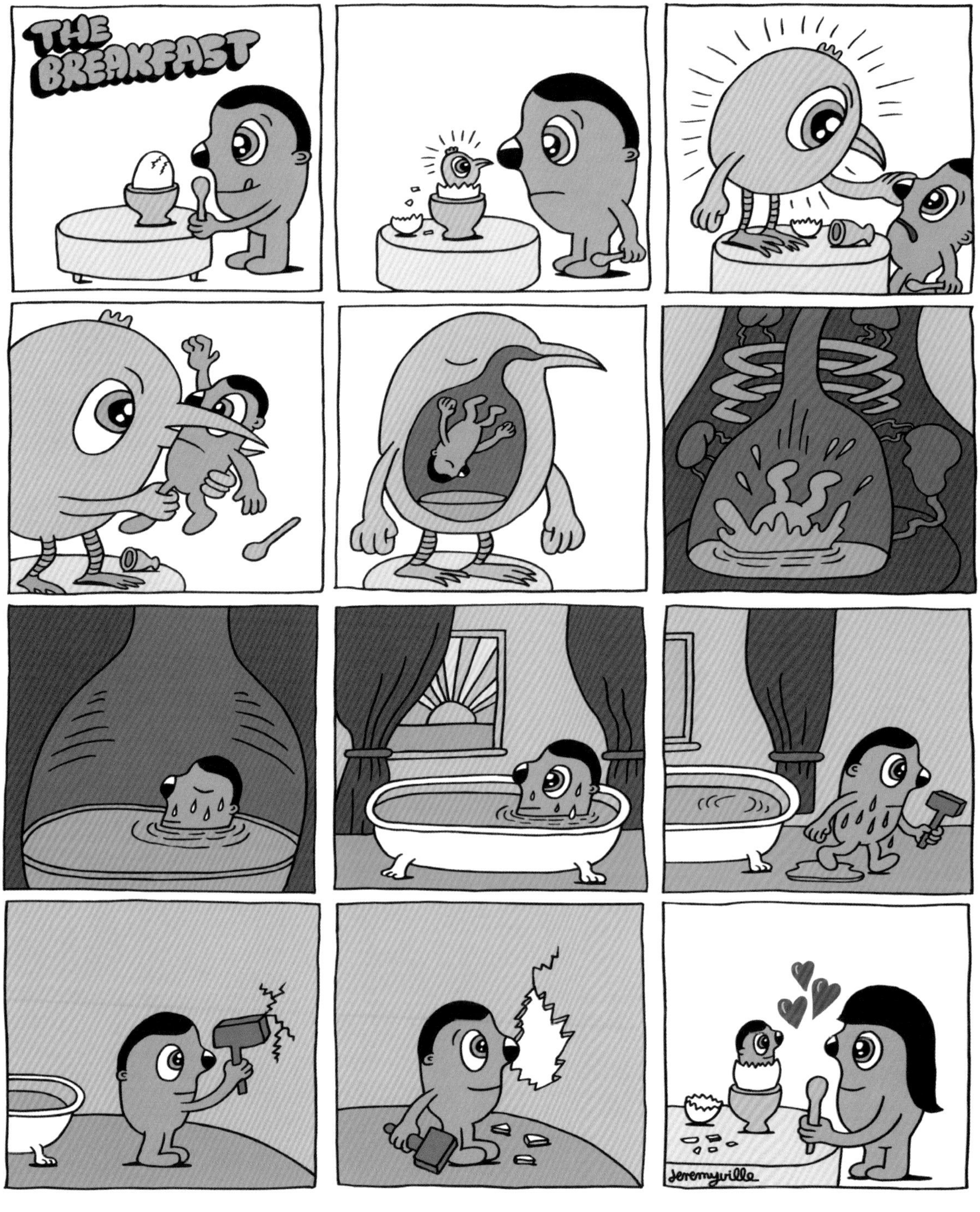
THE BREAKFAST
jeremyville

254"

jeremyville

jeremyville
PETTING ZOO

DESIGN LAB
Vinyl Will Kill!
CONTAINS:
1 designer toy poster
56 web cards
232 page book

jeremyville
SESSIONS
an inside look at COLLABORATIONS
with over 300 international artists
and companies
from the author of
Vinyl Will Kill !

HOUSTON ST.
GHOST OF ANDY
FREEDOM
BUY
GIANT CORP.
SUBWAY SIGHS
CANAL ST.
BROADWAY
TIMES
NY
FOOT LONG
NOHO
NOLITA
SPRING ST
BAGELS
LATTE
KEEP IT REAL ESTATE
LAFAYETTE
ESPRESSO...
SPOILT
BAGUETTE & CO.
LITTLE ITALY

Toy cube

A spontaneous artist, Keith Poon, originally from Hong Kong, now locates himself in New York.

He's been designing for 5 years, and considers himself mainly a 3D design lover, "I enjoy seeing and working in 3 dimensions. I like being able to physically manipulate my creations and touch them."

Keith usually bases his ideas upon what he likes, and with zodiac and aquatic life being some of his main interests. "The Kanizas are the mini-series figures that I had designed based on the original Kanser figure. Since the hermit crab changes shells, I created new types of shells which correspond with various types of fish. There are heads of a boxfish, hammerhead shark, squid and starfish. Finally, the Sharkys shown here were created because I like sharks. I like the movie Jaws and feel that sharks are very misunderstood. I wanted to show how sharks could be cute and mean (with and without blood)."

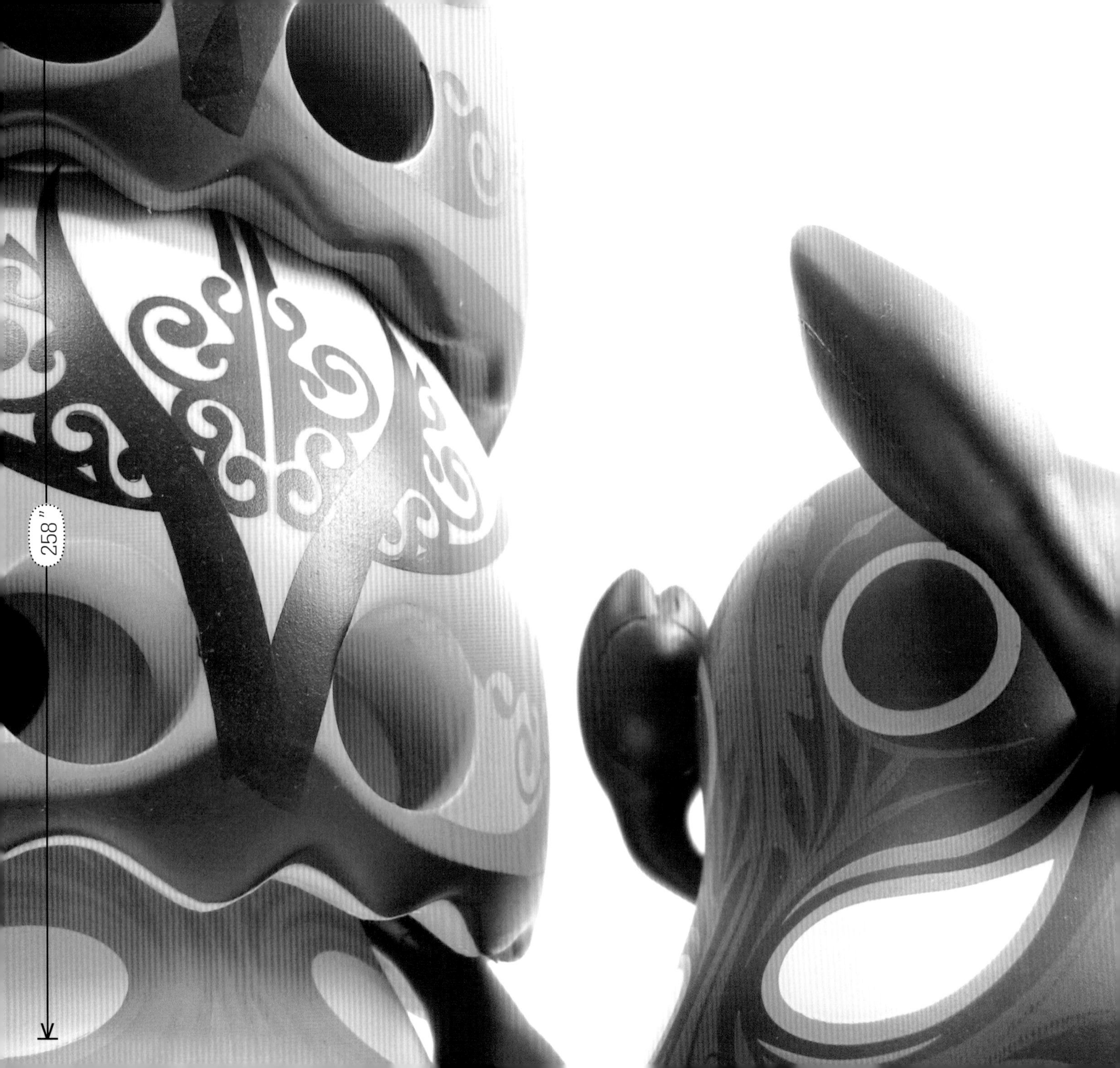

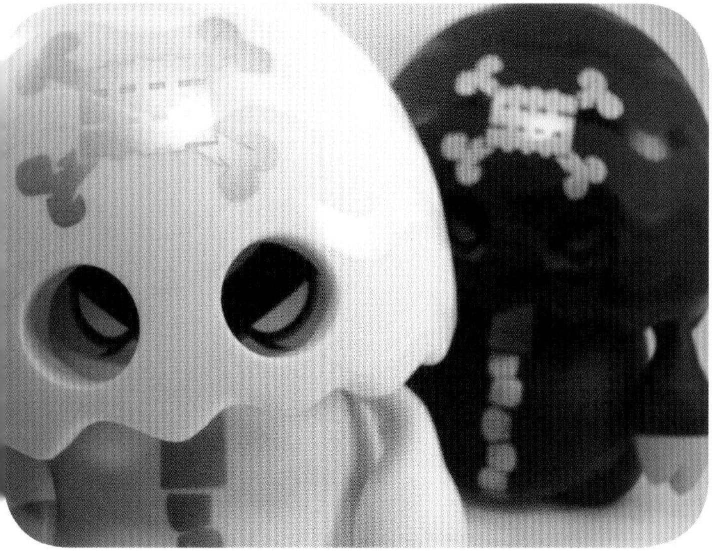

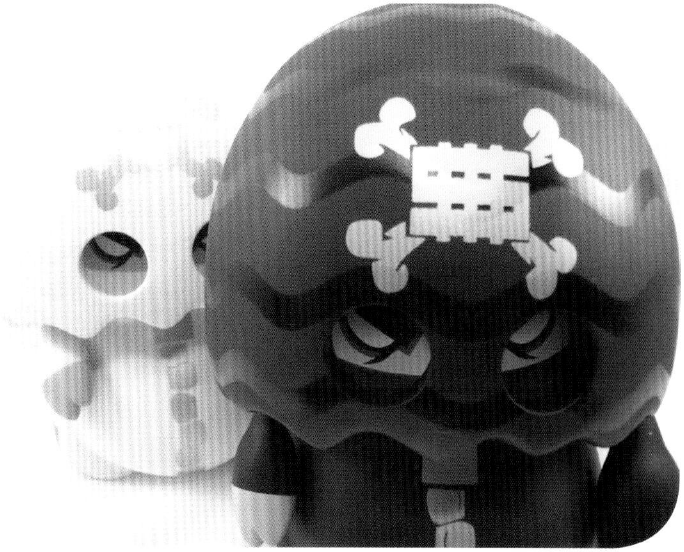

BREATHING OXYGEN
4500 PSI

What's The Skinny

Clients and projects you last worked on?

I have worked on several projects with popular artists. There were collaborations with graffiti artist Futura and Jakuan of the 360ToyGroup. Andrew Bell and MAD! have both worked on my Kanser figure. Several artists have also done designs on my Kaniza figures, like Simone Legno (Tokidoki), FILTH and Julie West. Huck Gee and Frank Kozik have done Sharky designs for me. I've also done several customs for various shows, using the Trexi.

What do you enjoy about your work?

I enjoy all the aspects of my work. I like the brain-storming and the design work. It is really exciting to create something new. My favorite part of my work is when I see the 3D models of my designs. The whole process is very invigorating. I also enjoy when I see the reactions to my toys and my products. I am happy when they like what I've produced and share their feelings about them to me.

Where do you find your inspiration?

I find inspiration in everything around me. My surroundings are my inspiration.

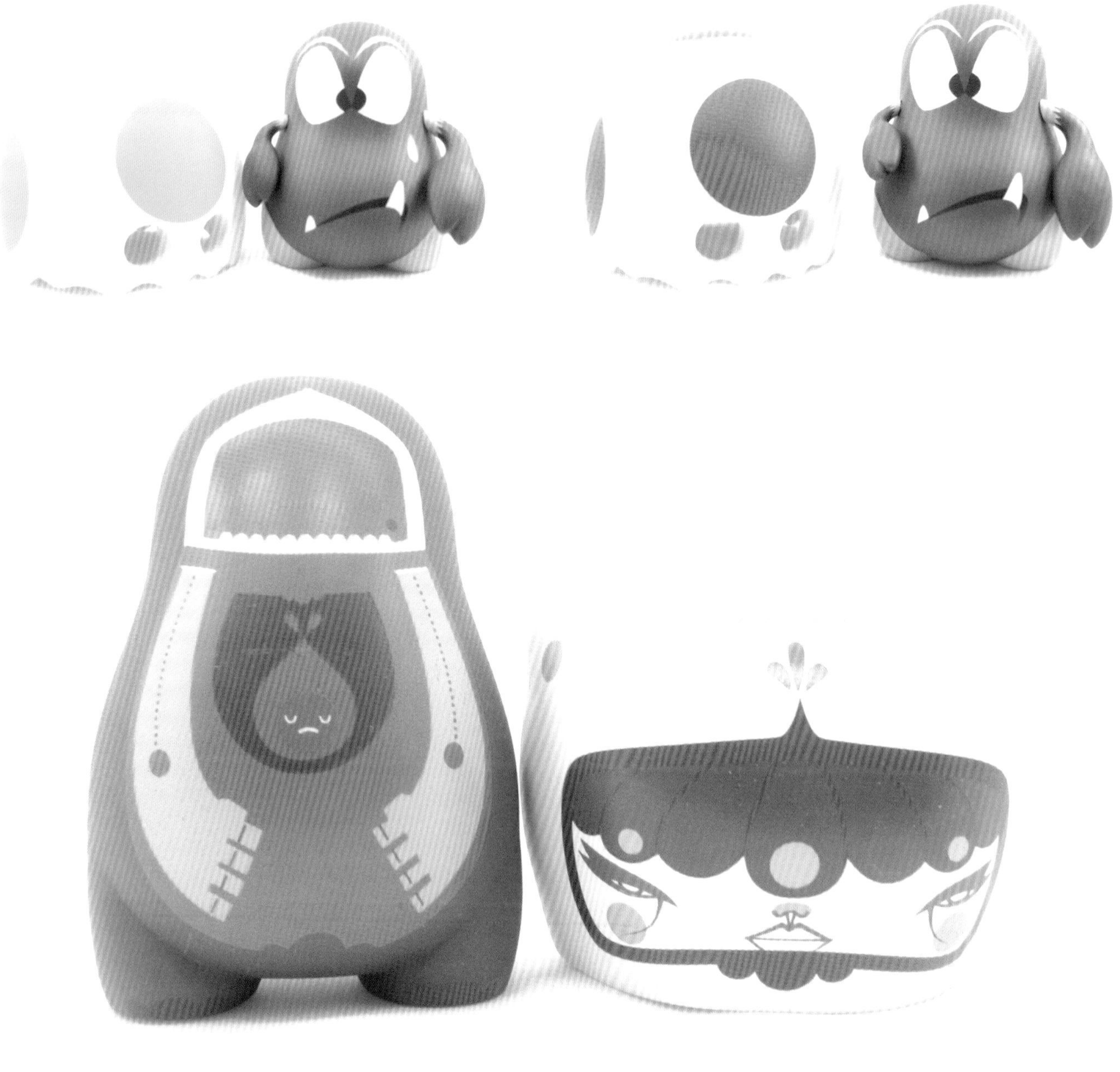

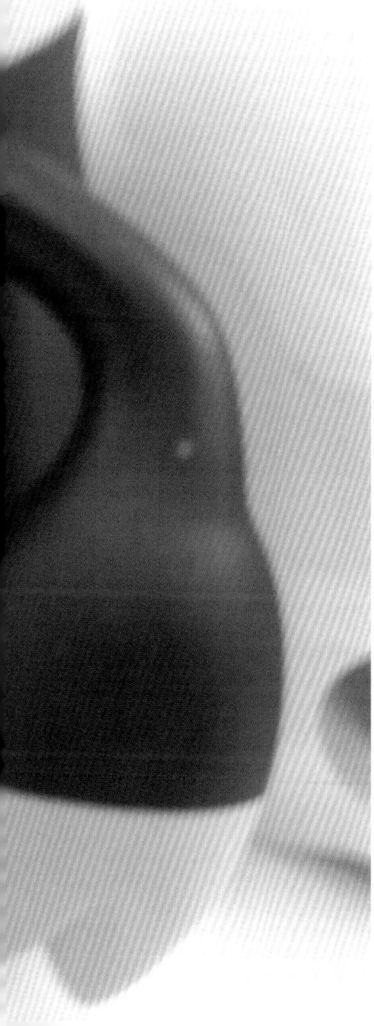

DANGER
DANGER

DANGER

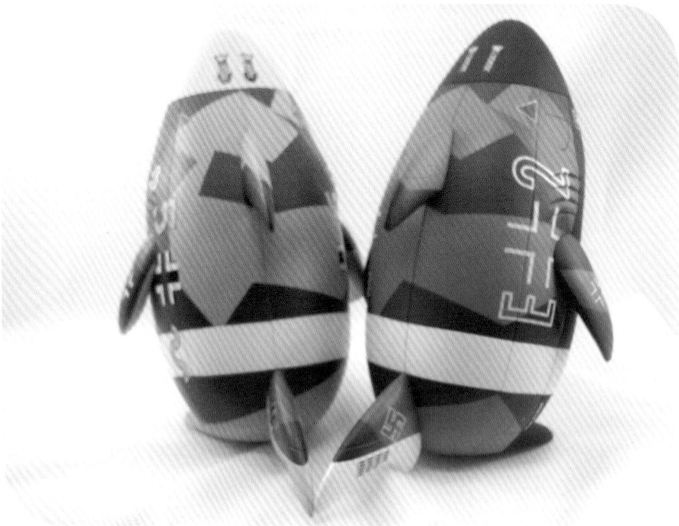

273 "

274"

TOY

DANGER
DANGER

TOY

Huck Gee

Having moved to San Francisco 15 years ago to pursue his art, Huck Gee seems to have succeeded. This artist from England, now has his own studio and is in high demand all over the world, for his work both as an illustrator and toy designer. His favorite media to work with are toys and canvas.

Surprising though, is where this artist gets his inspiration from... "driving fast and chasing skirts"! But perhaps, this shows us just how unconfined Huck Gee likes to be, having broken into the fashion industry as well as his usual fields. He recently launched a line of jewelry with Random Nature and has his own clothing line in production.

Owner of a vivid imagination and the famous pencil #2, Huck Gee is ready to create. And as he tells us, "being bad-ass and inspiring others" still stays as his main aim, "apart from world domination, of course!"

"There are no rules. Do what you love, the rest will follow."

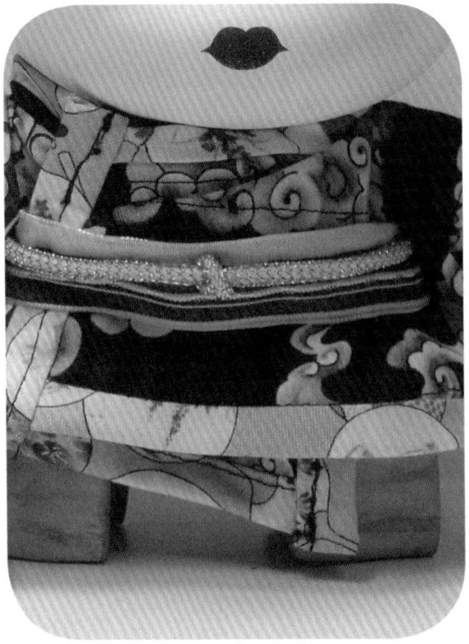

命

T051973
DANGER
AKUMABOMB

What's The Skinny

Clients and projects you last worked on?

Kidrobot, ToyQube, Fresh Manila, Toy2R, Play Imaginative, CircusPunks, DJ Qbert, Everlast, Barneys, The Standard Hotel, Advan/Yokohama, LIC Motorsports, Subydude, Subiesport Magazine, and Playstation Magazine to name a few.

What do you enjoy about your work?

I thoroughly enjoy the community I am involved in. Such an amazing and inspiring group of artists and downright honestly good natured peeps.

Where do you find your inspiration?

I find inspiration everywhere.

284"
命
金命

死
命

死

love
hate

hate

love

13

死

SUBARU
subaru-global.com
PIRELLI
HG WRC
prodrive
MOTUL

DENSO
PIAA
PIRELLI
SUBARU

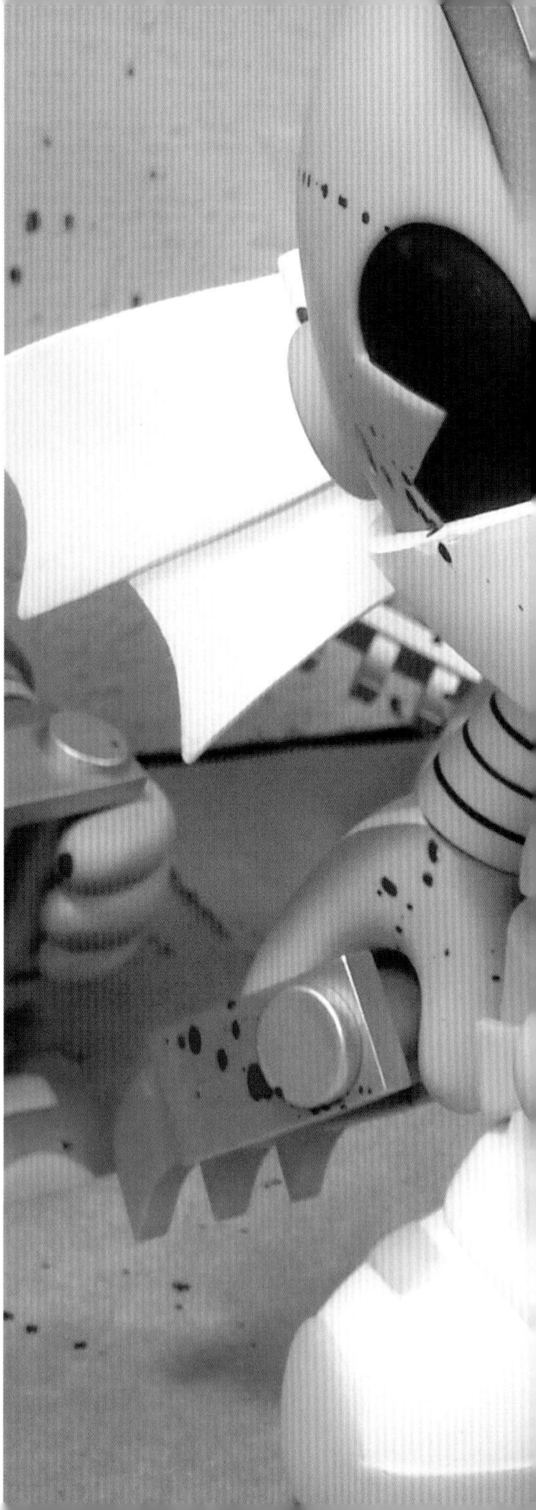

KRYLON
Primer

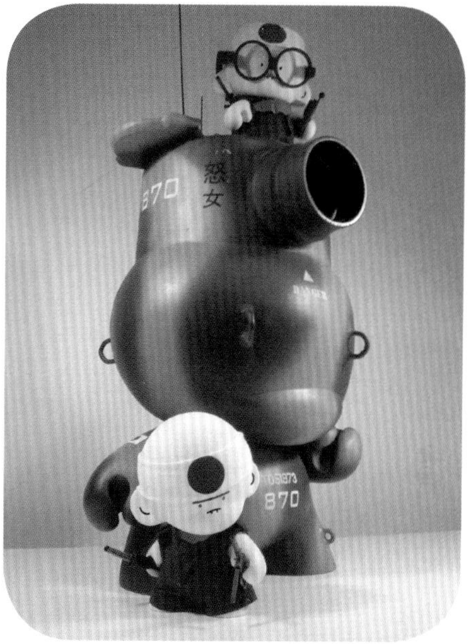

297"

DANGER

LUCKY
SUZIE

13
T051973

13
13
T051973

命
死
Mama's Boy
OVER

死
死
Mama's Boy

GAME
OVER

命
死
死
Mama's Boy
GAME

Mama's Boy

kidrobot
:BANANA:
ホアック ジー
http://www.huckgee.com
OMGHI2U!

Geordie
Racing
Huck Gee

kidrobot
ホアック ジー
OMGHI2U!

ホアック ジー
死

HELLO
my name is
HELL
my name
死

HELLO
I'm insAne

¡HOLA!
mi llamo es

my name is
HELLO
my name is
HELLO
my name is

HELLO
my name is
HELLO
my name is
HELLO
my name is

Life

XXX

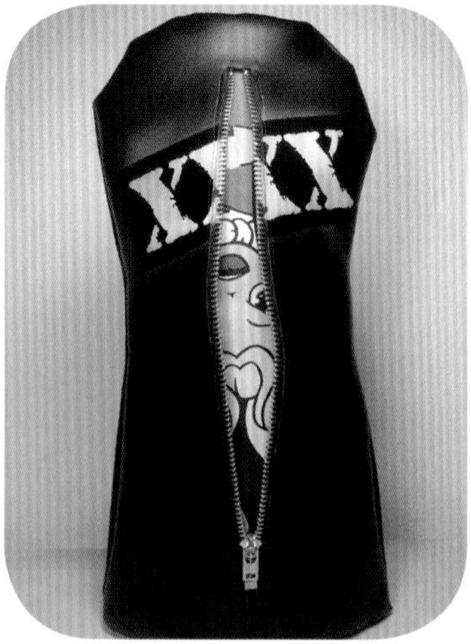

死
ホアックジー
HG

死
死

SAVED
SAVE HUCK

死
死
死

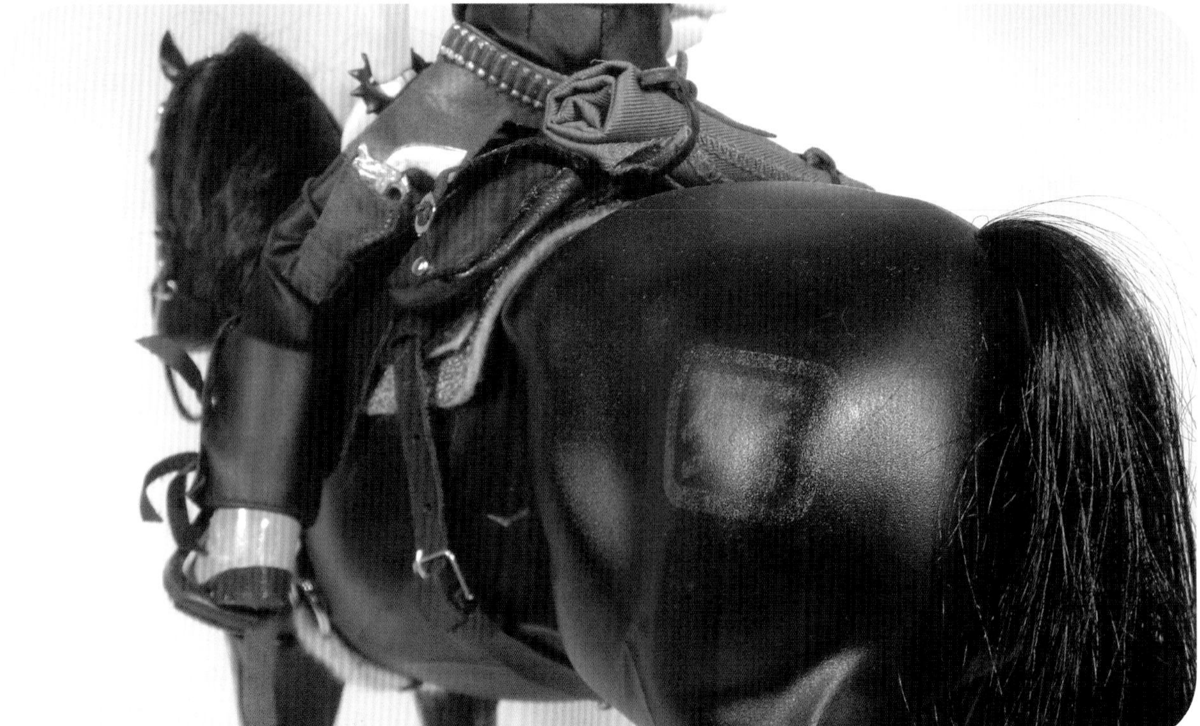

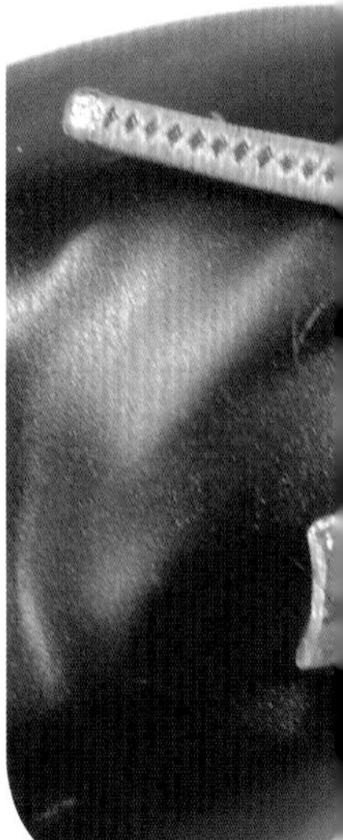

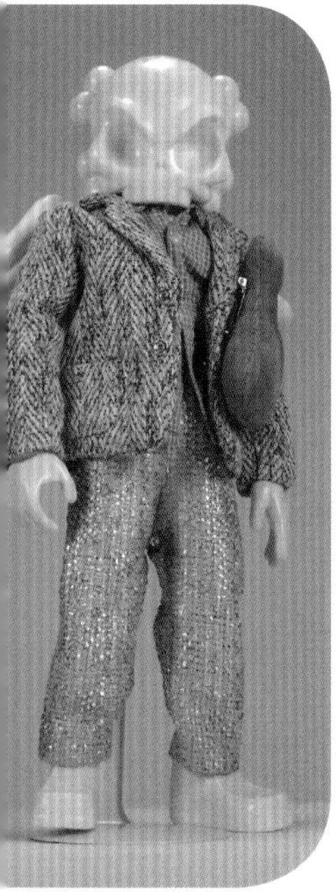

13
HUMGEE

死

死

TO51973
13
TO51973
DANGER

Marka27

The minigods are the latest manifestation from the restless mind of Marka27, the first indigenous urban vinyl.

Maka27 is currently collaborating with "B.I.C Plastics" on his new graffiti inspired urban vinyl 8" figure "Killa Instinct" His graffiti has been seen in high profile galleries throughout the east and west coast and has shown along side artists such as Futura, and Sam Flores.

His street murals/ graffiti have been published in several life style magazines and books, most recently "Graffiti Planet,""Burning New York," and "Graffiti L.A."

Marka27 made his mark with his original "Audio Canvas" paintings with built in speakers, also his large speaker installations with legendary hiphop icons painted on the speaker boxes.

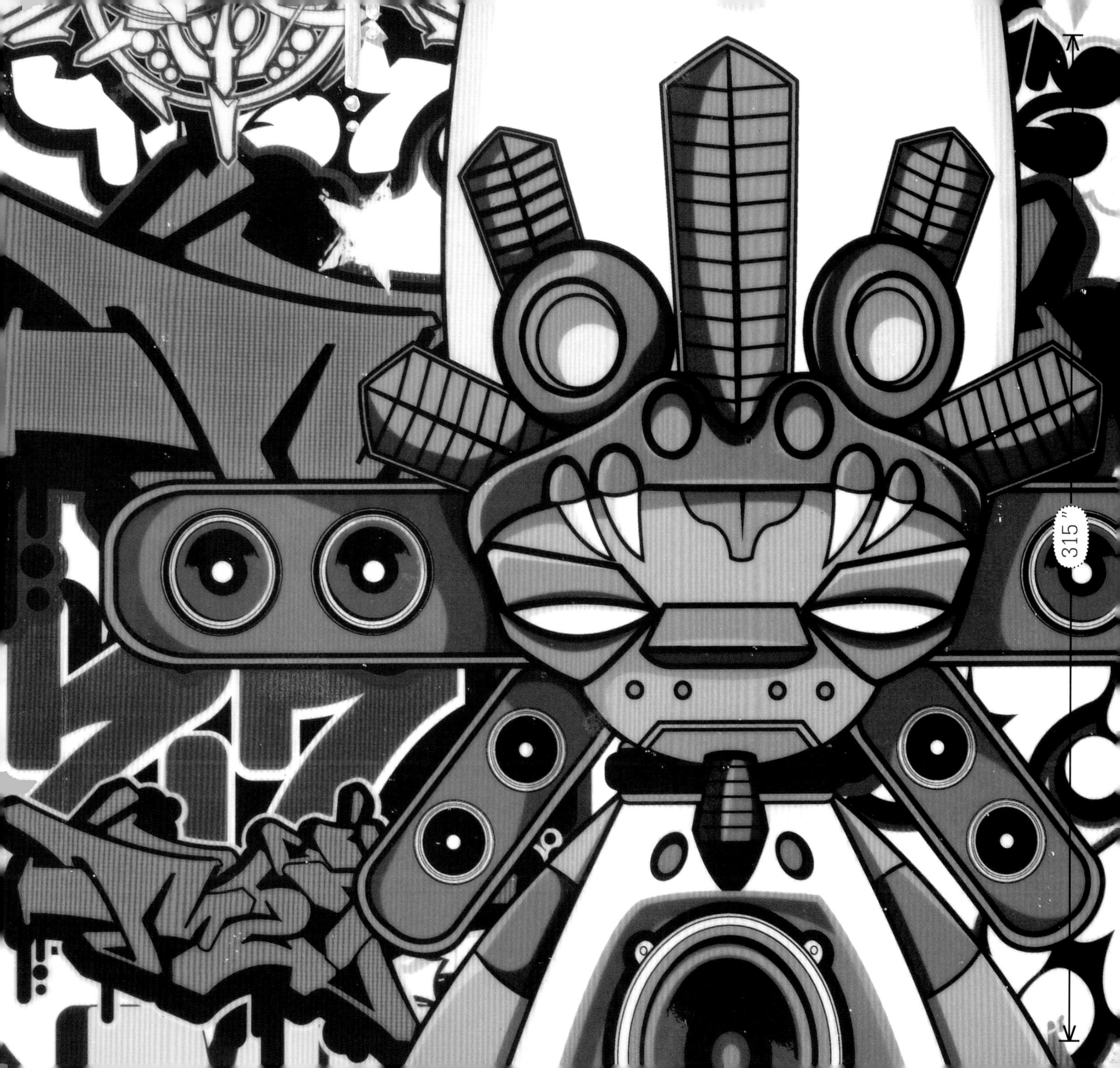

Index

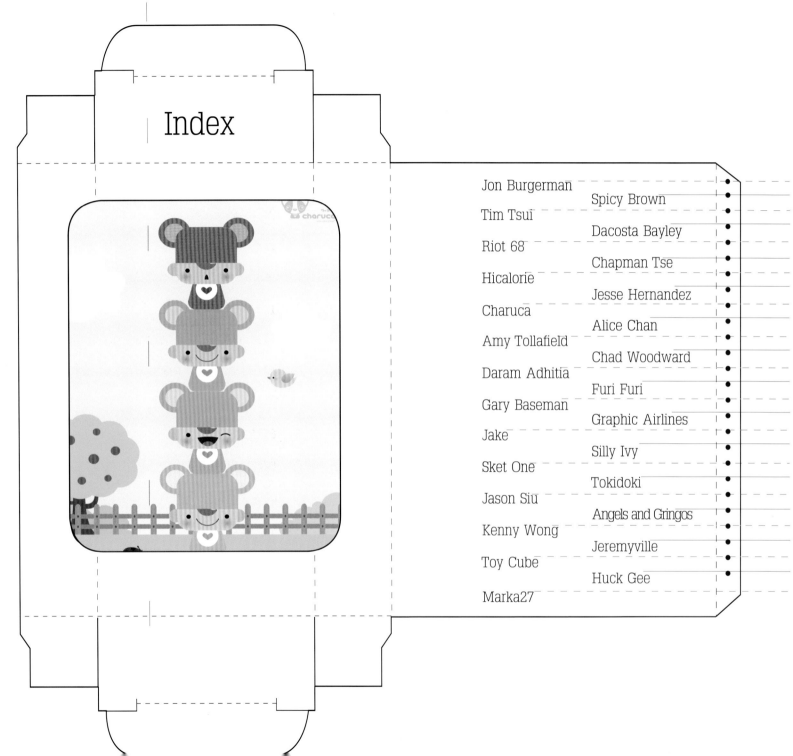

www.spicybrown.com / scott@spicybrown.com

www.chocolatesoop.com / info@chocolatesoop.com

www.yellowatelier.com / chap@yellowatelier.com

www.immortalstudios.net / immortalstudios@hotmail.com

www.asterialand.com / info@asterialand.com

www.chadwoodward.com / chadwoodward@hotmail.com

www.furifuri.com / info@furifuri.com

www.graphicairlines.com / mail@graphicairlines.com

www.sillyivy.com / sillyivy@163.com

www.tokidoki.it / simone@tokidoki.it

www.angelsandgringos.com / info@angelsandgringos.com

www.jeremyville.com / jeremy@jeremyville.com

www.huckgee.com / info@huckgee.com

www.jonburgerman.com / jon@jonburgerman.com

www.teamzero.com.hk / info@teamzero.com.hk

www.riot68.com / riot68@riot68.com

www.hicalorie.com / alex@hicalorie.com

www.charuca.net / charuca@charuca.net

www.amytollafield.com /amytollafield@hotmail.co.uk

www.thedarbotz.com / darbotz@gmail.com

www.garybaseman.com / info@garybaseman.com

www.jake-art.com / jakesteel@btinternet.com

www.sket-one.com / sket@sket-one.com

www.jasonsiu.com / info@jasonsiu.com

www.kennyswork.com / info@kennyswork.com

www.toyqube.com / info@toyqube.com

www.marka27.com / 27marka@gmail.com

First Published by Gingko Press in the United States of America in 2009
by arrangement with Liaoning Science and Technology Publishing House

First Edition
Gingko Press, Inc.
1321 Fifth Street
Berkeley, CA 94710, USA

Phone (510) 898 1195
Fax (510) 898 1195
www.gingkopress.com

ISBN: 978-1-58423-334-3

Editor and designer: Shawn Wright
Associate editor: Brigida Neves

Printed in China